Percy Bysshe Shelley, Joseph Skipsey

Lyrics and Minor Poems

Percy Bysshe Shelley, Joseph Skipsey

Lyrics and Minor Poems

ISBN/EAN: 9783744712330

Printed in Europe, USA, Canada, Australia, Japan

Cover: Foto ©Thomas Meinert / pixelio.de

More available books at **www.hansebooks.com**

The J. C. Saul Collection
of
Nineteenth Century
English Literature

Purchased in part
through a contribution to the
Library Funds made by the
Department of English in
University College.

THE LYRICS AND MINOR POEMS

OF

PERCY BYSSHE SHELLEY.

[SELECTED]

With a Prefatory Notice, Biographical
and Critical.

BY

JOSEPH SKIPSEY.

 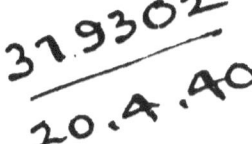

LONDON
Walter Scott, 24 Warwick Lane, Paternoster Row
AND NEWCASTLE-ON-TYNE
1887

PR
6403
S5

CONTENTS.

	Page
Prefatory Notice	9
Alastor; or, The Spirit of Solitude	33
To Coleridge	57
Stanzas—April 1814	58
Mutability	60
On Death	60
A Summer-Evening Churchyard	62
To Wordsworth	63
Feelings of a Republican on the fall of Bonaparte	64
Lines (The cold Earth slept below)	64
The Sunset	66
Hymn to Intellectual Beauty	68
Mont Blanc	71
Julian and Maddalo	76

CONTENTS.

	Page
Marianne's Dream	97
Death	102
To Constantia, Singing	103
Sonnet—Ozymandias	104
To the Lord Chancellor	105
To William Shelley	107
Lines (That time is dead for ever, child)	109
On Fanny Godwin	110
Lines to a Critic	110
Passage of the Apennines	112
On a Dead Violet	113
The Past	113
Sonnet (Lift not the painted veil)	114
Lines written among the Euganean Hills	114
Stanzas (The sun is warm, the sky is clear)	126
Misery	128
The Witch of Atlas	131
The Masque of Anarchy	154
Lines (Corpses are cold in the tomb)	167
Song—To the Men of England	168
England in 1819	170
Similes for Two Political Characters of 1819	170

CONTENTS.

	Page
God Save the Queen	171
Ode to the Asserters of Liberty	173
Ode to Heaven	174
Ode to the West Wind	176
An Exhortation	179
The Indian Serenade	180
Lines written for Miss Sophia Stacey	181
Epipsychidion	182
Love's Philosophy	203
Ode to Liberty	204
Arethusa	213
Hymn of Apollo	216
Hymn of Pan	218
The Question	219
The Sensitive Plant	221
The Cloud	232
To a Skylark	235
To ——. (I fear thy kisses, gentle maiden)	239
The Two Spirits	239
Song of Proserpine	241
Letter to Maria Gisborne	242
Ode to Naples	252
Summer and Winter	258

CONTENTS.

	Page
Lines to a Reviewer	259
Autumn.—A Dirge	259
Liberty	260
The Tower of Famine	261
Time long past	262
Good-night	262
Sonnet (Ye hasten to the dead)	263
Adonais	264
Dirge for the year	282
To Night	283
From the Arabic	284
Song (Rarely, rarely comest thou)	285
To Emilia Viviani	287
Lines (Far, far away)	287
Time	288
A Song	288
Ariel to Miranda	289

Prefatory Notice.

F the mighty singer who produced the immortal poems contained in this volume—Shelley,—that "pard-like spirit, beautiful and swift," a few words, and a few words only, by way of preface. Percy Bysshe Shelley was the eldest son of Mr. (afterwards Sir) Timothy and Elizabeth Shelley, and was born at Field Place, near Horsham, Sussex, on the 4th of August 1792. "He was a beautiful boy," says his excellent critic and biographer, Mr. W. M. Rossetti, "with ringlets, deep blue eyes, a snowy complexion and exquisitely formed hands and feet," and he was remarkable for his gentleness and sweetness of disposition. From childhood he was in the highest degree sensitive, and too keenly alive to all

discordant influences, physical and mental, to feel at all at ease in mixed and unruly companies. Mere clownishness of manners he could put up with, but coarseness of lauguage and sordidness of disposition excited his disgust; and of this he had more than enough at Sion House School, Brentford, to which he was sent when he was about ten years old. "The pupils here were mostly boys," says Mr. Rossetti, "numbering about sixty, sons of local tradesmen; the system of the house was mean," and the reception accorded to Shelley by his school-fellows, and their subsequent treatment of him, "full of taunting and petty persecution." Girlish in appearance and averse to rough sports, he was naturally enough deemed a proper butt for the jibes of the ruder boys; and notwithstanding the fact that, when thoroughly aroused, he would display a courage and determination, before which the boldest of his juvenile opponents for the moment would quail—such a butt he was so often made as to make his "situation one of acute misery." The effect of this upon his after-career was clearly enormous, since he was forced at the very outset of his life to have a powerful dislike for human haunts—for the actual and the real; and had his soul not been formed of the very essence of love, he, in all

PREFATORY NOTICE. 11

likelihood, had sunk into a mere sneerer and a man-hater. This, thank God, he could not become; and the more he suffered the more he only felt for others who suffered likewise, and the more he was impelled to seek out a remedy for the evils of which he and they were the victims. In this search the painful fact burst upon his young mind, that the evils of which he complained were only a specimen of what dominated the world at large, and that only could be a panacea for the one which should embrace the whole. And how was that to be effected? By a moral warfare, in which he and no other should be the hero! "And from that hour" he afterwards sang :—

> "And from that hour did I with earnest thought
> Heap knowledge from forbidden mines of lore,
> Yet nothing that my tyrants knew or taught,
> I cared to learn—but from that secret store
> Wrought linked armour for my soul before
> It might go forth to war among mankind."

Thus while yet a boy in years he foresaw, and began to prepare for the struggle—the intellectual war against social, political, and religious wrong—that in later years he was to enter into, and which was to last till the hour of his death. Shelley's career, with some brief intervals of quietude and joy, was indeed one of pain and strife from the cradle to the grave. A moral hero he was if there ever was one, and when we consider the purity of his motives, and, in general, the nobleness of the objects—truth, justice, and freedom—for which he always strove, it would not be too much to say that he merits the respect of the good and the wise, apart from any honour due to him for the many immortal poems he has left behind for our wonder and delight. In his fourteenth year he went to Eton, where, besides studying the Greek and Roman classics, for which, we are told, he had an especial capacity, he was soon found to be also a student of "mines of forbidden lore." "He studied the occult sciences, watched for spectres, conjured the devil, and speculated on a visit to Africa," says Mr. Rossetti, "for the purpose of searching out the magic arcana which her dusky populations are noted for." Of course this could only be accounted for on the supposition that the youth had a hopelessly perverse disposition—if, indeed, he was not mad. So deemed the graver Etonians, and many freaks are related that had half justified their suspicions, had the rich produce of his gifts not been left to show that, however unusual his conduct may have appeared, such eccentricity was only the natural result of a great inner force—a genius in this case of an almost incomprehensible magnitude—seeking, and, as yet, seeking in vain for an expression. This the Etonians did not understand, and so felt themselves justified in treating the girlish-faced youth with even a greater degree of harshness and rudeness than it had been his misfortune to endure at Sion House—though this they were not always allowed to do with impunity. If the youth was not mad, the cruelty to which he was so often subjected was enough to make him so; and we are not surprised on being told that, in a fit of rage caused by some impish persecution on a certain occasion, "he stuck a penknife through the offender's hand." For this offence we are left to suppose that he was expelled from Eton; and are informed that he had been twice expelled before. If this be true—for the truth of the statement is doubted—then the more shame to the Eton authorities for not having taken steps to put an end to the persecution which resulted in the scenes of which they complained. The agony which drove the youth to so act must have been great indeed, and the effect of its relation becomes doubly painful when we learn that, amid all this, he was attacked by a brain fever, during which he was only saved from being sent to a madhouse by the interposition of a Dr. Lind, "who posted to Field Place," at the poet's request, "satisfied his father" as to the state of affairs, and "cured him" of his affliction. A silver lining is afforded to the black cloud which hung over our poet at this period through the intelligent sympathy of this good doctor. "He loved me," said Shelley, "and I shall never forget our long talks, where he breathed the spirit of kindest tolerance and the purest wisdom." All honour then to the doctor, for what immense debt may we not all owe him for the beneficial results of these "long talks!" Another drop of honey was let fall into Shelley's cup of gall about this time through a certain tender feeling he had wakened in the heart of his cousin, Harriet Grove. "He loved her," it is said, "and she returned his affections." They corresponded and were to marry; yet I venture to say that the love on one side was rather pity for the sufferings of the other, and the love on the other was rather a deep sense of thankfulness at his having found one—and that one of the gentler sex—who could appreciate his troubles, than that passion which in the highest sense can only be called love, and which melts and fuses two souls into one. Generosity or selfishness may cause two human beings to be put together as man and wife, but the passion here spoken of, and that only, can sanctify the marriage knot. This the world does not understand, and won't try, and broken hearts are the consequence; the grey-headed too often laugh the sacredness of the passion to scorn, and even the young are far from being able at all times to set it at its proper value. Even Shelley in his early youth failed to do so. Chivalric feelings or brotherly and sisterly affection were mistaken for the celestial fire, and hence his errors in this way. At a later period no one had ever a clearer conception of the matter, and instead of a promise of marriage, a feeling like that which existed between him and his cousin Harriet would have found ventilation in song, and so have ended, only at the time he left Eton his song gift was not in blossom. Shelley's genius, by the way, could not be said to have had a premature development; none of his literary efforts up to the time he left Eton are held to possess much merit. This was in the year 1809. In 1810 he went to Oxford, from whence he was expelled in 1811 for what was deemed a much graver offence than any that had been laid to his charge at Eton—viz., that of printing and causing to be circulated a pamphlet entitled, *The Necessity for Atheism.* In the same year he married—not the cousin Harriet just mentioned, but Harriet Westbrook, a school-girl of sixteen, and a retired hotel-keeper's daughter.

Of all the misfortunes that ever befell Shelley, that of his early death excepted, this marriage was by far the greatest. Harriet Grove, out of sympathy for Shelley's sufferings, had at one time thought herself sufficiently in love to have been justified in becoming his wife; Shelley in a similar way, out of pity for certain troubles of Harriet Westbrook, had been induced to become her husband. "Harriet was not only delightful to look at," says Mr. Rossetti, "but altogether most agreeable. She dressed with exquisite neatness and propriety; her voice was pleasant and her speech cordial; her spirits were cheerful and her manners good." She was withal, "well-educated," a "pleasant reader," and well skilled in music. Surely with such a woman the best of men—and Shelley was one of the best of men—might have lived, one would naturally have thought, on the best of terms? And for a short time he did so; then—the world has long known what afterwards befell, and the reason of the dire calamity lay in the fact that Shelley had mistaken pity for something else, and that `in reality he had never truly loved the woman he had taken to be his wife. His error was a huge one, and the cooling down of his affection, then discord, then separation, then suicide on the wife's part, was the consequence. The weakest in this case, as in others, went to the wall; but let it not for a moment be supposed that the strongest passed on unscathed. An avenging Nemesis followed the young poet's footsteps to the end, and the furies of Regret, Remorse, and Shame threw their raven shadow o'er his life, and his soul—at least so long as it remained tagged to his frail body—his "soul from out that shadow was lifted nevermore!" Such at least is my conviction, and I would hail with delight any reliable account that would lead me to a happier conclusion. I do not think that Shelley was guilty of any wilful wrong, but the gravity of the errors he committed in his marriage of, and then separation from, Harriet, leading as they did to the most tragic consequences, were such as to smite his sensitive being to the centre; and if any proofs were wanting for this more than are afforded by the facts of his outer life, we have only to refer to his songs, which in Shelley's case were, even far more than the songs of Byron were in his, a veritable reflection of the inner man. His "sweetest songs" at all times were those which told of "saddest thought;" but after the tragical death of Harriet, and his union with Mary Godwin, with whom he had eloped on parting from Harriet, the sorrow of his songs, and more especially of his greatest ones, grew deeper

* B

and deeper. The surprising fecundity of his
genius after his second marriage is ascribed in
some measure to the harmony which prevailed
between him and his second wife, and this
too may have been without at all affecting the
truth of my intimations. Poetry is an art as
well as an inspiration, and quietude and social
harmony are among the essentials for its success-
ful cultivation; but these may exist while the soul
itself is carried away through the force of bitter
memories to "look on the past and stare aghast at
the spectres wailing pale and ghast, of hopes which
thou and I beguiled to death on life's dark river!"
What a sigh! and what a world of pain and
mental torment are discovered by these few words
in inverted commas, and yet these are from a lyric
penned in 1817, and when he was the husband of
his truly beloved Mary Godwin. Without casting
any aspersions on poor Harriet—for in years she
was only a girl (and he was little more than a boy)—
during her connection with Shelley, it ought to be
said, however, that it is some credit to Mary that
our bard's genius found a free, high, and triumphant expression under her care. During his
connection with Harriet he had produced his first
great effort in verse, the "Queen Mab," but after
his second marriage every succeeding year had its

immortal product. First of that glorious progeny came "Alastor," 1816 ; then the "Revolt of Islam," 1817; then the "Rosalind and Helen," and "Julian and Maddalo" both 1818; then "The Cenci," 1819; the "Witch of Atlas" and the "Prometheus Unbound," 1820 ; the "Epipsychidion," the "Adonais," and the "Hellas," all in 1821 ; and he was engaged on other works when death by drowning put an end to his career on the 4th of July 1822. Such a career! Besides the great poems named, he, during the same wonderful period, poured forth a flood of lyrics and lesser pieces which in themselves had won for him a rank only second to the highest in literature. The great poems named raise him among those who occupy the highest rank. In many of his pieces he displayed too strong a predilection for the merely fanciful, but his greatest efforts are noted beyond those of all other poets since Milton for the magnificent and the sublime. In sublimity he was only surpassed by Milton and Shakespeare, and "no, nobody," says Leigh Hunt, "had a style so Orphic. His poetry is so full of mountains, seas, and skies, of light and darkness, and the seasons, and all the elements of our being, as if Nature herself had written it with the creation and its hopes newly cast around her ; but it must be confessed not without too indiscriminate a mixture of great and small, and a want of sufficient shade—a certain chaotic brilliancy, 'dark with excess of light.'" Besides this fault, which arises out of a plethora of fancy, there is another which is the offspring of an excessive fondness for knotty mental problems and subjects which rather belong to the sphere of the metaphysician than that of the poet, and in the treatment of which he necessarily discarded the example and precept of Milton, who held that poetry ought to be "simple, sensous, and passionate"—or "impassioned," as Coleridge has it—and both of these defects infect even the very greatest of his productions—"The Cenci" excepted. These charges may be brought especially and most emphatically against the "Prometheus Unbound," and yet in despite of all, this must be conceded to be one of the most marvellous poems in the language! The conception of this drama, and more especially of the characters of the hero, and of Asia, and Panthea, are worthy of Milton, though the execution in detail and throughout is not equal to what we would have expected in a similar work from the hand of that mighty master. If not as a whole, however, yet in long passages, even in the dialogue, he equals the best poets when at their best; while in his choral strains he rises far above what any poet had ever in a similar way attempted before. A yet higher encomium by many of our ablest critics is pronounced upon "The Cenci." Many declare it to be the best drama we have had since the Elizabethan era, and some even regard it quite as a Shakespearean one. It is a great drama, but it is not Shakespearean. Shelley found in the magic mirror of his imagination, indeed, the various characters reflected in his verse; yet if these were not merely reflections of himself they were all too much coloured by his own feelings to be Shakespearean. The Prince of Dramatists undoubtedly, like all other poets, must have incorporated much of his own personality into his creations, since, as Blake has it, "It is impossible to thought a greater than itself to know;" but his genius was too supreme to allow this to be seen—or be traceable! With Shelley, as with Milton, the case was otherwise. "In the 'Paradise Lost,'" says Coleridge, "indeed, in every one of his poems, it is Milton himself whom you see: his Satan, his Raphael, almost his Eve, are all John Milton." And in a similar way, may be said, that nearly all Shelley's characters are in some measure a reproduction of himself. Set aside the consideration of sex, even the charming Beatrice, in "The

Cenci," is so. That great poem may be none the worse on that account—only it is not Shakespearean. Shakespeare is often spoken of as being "many-sided." He would be better represented, however, by a circle than a polygon, everything touched by which is touched at a point equi-distant from the centre; but not so would be such a genius as Shelley or Milton, though both of these rare poets were also, though in a less degree, many-sided, and each in his way gives us a series of characters tender and beautiful, lofty and sublime. Many of these are painted to the life. Those of "The Cenci" are especially so, and the story of that drama is well told. "In all probability," as Mr. Devey observes in his magnificent essay upon Shelley, "in Shakespeare's hands the plot of 'The Cenci' would have assumed a wider basis. The facetious element would have been introduced in which Shelley was wofully deficient;" but when he, nevertheless, adds that "he hardly thinks the story would have been better told," I fail to see the logic of his conclusions. In Shakespeare's hands the story would have been differently told, though whether more effectively is another question; but surely had he felt the necessity of introducing the "facetious element" (and I presume he would not have introduced it without feeling that necessity), the story would most surely have been better for its introduction. But the work as Shelley has given it is a master-piece, and few can read it without wishing that he had given us many such. And had he lived longer it is just possible that he might have done so, and yet is it likely that he would? One must admit that this is questionable. Of this one thing we are certain, no sooner had he put the finishing touch to "The Cenci," than he set about writing another poem—"The Witch of Atlas"—in which he returns to the purely ideal with all the rapture with which an eagle that has escaped from a trap might be supposed to return to his aery in the regions of the sun. The effect of this upon his noble-minded wife, who was one of his best critics, was such as to draw from her an animadversion, and to which in turn he playfully replied with the verses commencing :—

> " How, my dear Mary, are you critic-bitten
>   (For vipers kill, though dead) by some review,
> That you condemn these verses I have written,
>   Because they tell no story, false or true?
> What though no mice are caught by a young kitten,
>   May it not leap and play as grown cats do,
> Till its claws come? Prithee, for this one time
> Content thee with a visionary rhyme."

But Mary evidently thought that the kitten had

already had sufficient play—that it was all blarney about its claws not being grown, since it had just, at least, caught one very large mouse; or, to be more serious, that she and the world had already had too many visionary rhymes, and that this was the more to be lamented, since the mighty genius who had penned these rhymes had already displayed a capacity for the tragic drama such as had not been witnessed for ages. Regrets like these, though natural enough on his noble-minded wife's part, are, however, futile. Shelley, who at this very period, through causes before alluded to, was passing through the fiery furnace of regret and remorse, knew best what to him, for the time being, was his natural and best element; and when we reflect on what he achieved while in that element, we are awe-struck, abashed, and ashamed at our having been guilty of anything like fault-finding. We must take the great poet for what he was, not for what we in our blindness and weakness would wish him to have been, and in his own sphere he was a demi-god, and without a peer. "Out of the most indefinite terms of a hard, cold, dark, metaphysical system," says Macaulay, "he made a gorgeous Pantheon full of beautiful, majestic, and life-like forms. He turned Atheism itself into a mythology rich with visions as glorious as the gods that live in the marble of Phidias, or the virgin saints that smile on us from the canvas of Murillo." This being so, what more can we desire? What, indeed? Are we to find fault with the tree because, while it has yielded us a rich stock of grapes, it has not yielded us a rich stock of apples also? Grapes, however, are not, as we have seen, the truest symbols of Shelley's poems, although they all have a fair share of sweetness, and a few of the shorter pieces are laden with it. Subtlety of thought, gorgeousness of imagery—the magnificent or the sublime, linked to the most charming music, are the characteristics of his best work, and that *best* means the full half of his multitudinous and multifarious poems. Such are the dominant qualities of much of the "Revolt of Islam," "Alastor," "The Witch of Atlas," "The Adonais"—which poem is also steeped in deep spiritual pathos—and the other great poems before mentioned. "The Epipsychidion," the most impassioned of his narrative poems, is, indeed, a sort of celestial grape, and of such divine virtue, that once having touched our lips, we are set dreaming of visions of the most enchanting loveliness, and of love which satiates not for evermore! I was about to call this the most precious of all Shelley's precious poems, when lo, into my imagination comes the vision of The

Sensitive Plant, with its enchanted Garden and its Elf-like Lady Attendant, and anon is the question suggested, Can anything possibly be more precious than that? Most certainly there is nothing more original; and in honied sweetness, ethereal beauty, and in delicacy of workmanship and fairy-like melody united, I know of nothing to be compared with it out of Coleridge. That life-giving power of imagination which can only be possessed by the true poet, and which enabled him to create out of the most abstract terms the most life-like forms, as already spoken of, is exemplified in almost every verse in this glorious creation. Take as a specimen the opening stanza :—

> " A Sensitive Plant in a garden grew,
> And *the young winds fed it* with silver dew ;
> And *it opened its* fan-like *leaves to the light*,
> And *closed them beneath the kisses of night.*"

And again in another way :—

> " For Winter came ; *the wind was his whip ;*
> *One choppy finger was on his lip ;*
> *He had torn the cataracts from the hills,*
> *And they clanked at his girdle like manacles.*"

That, at least, is a personification of great power, and full of life, and yet it is perhaps excelled by his

PREFATORY NOTICE. 27

personification of Time in the "Mask of Anarchy." This other picture is painted in the words of a "maniac maid," the last survivor of the champions of Liberty which had been born to Time, and "whose name was Hope, though she looked more like Despair." Flying before the hideous revellers in the "Mask," she cries

> "My father Time is hoar and grey
> With waiting for a better day;
> See how idiot-like he stands,
> Fumbling with his palsied hands!
>
> He has had child after child,
> And the dust of death is piled
> Over every one but me—
> Misery—O, Misery!"

A fine subject for an artist that! but how is an artist to paint this?—

> "Revenge and wrong bring forth their kind,
> The foul cubs as their parent are;
> Their den is in the guilty mind,
> And conscience feeds them with despair."

This is from "Hellas," a lyrical drama, and a sublime song on behalf of Liberty. Shelley was always inspired and sublime when he sang of Liberty, and in his great odes, those to Naples and to Liberty in particular. His "Ode to the West

Wind" is also among his greatest things, and yet he is, perhaps, nowhere so fascinating as in those brief lyrics which come now like wild wails from the forest on the wings of the blast, and now like sighs on the fitful breeze from the reeds on the river brim. Not even "The Question," with its rich bouquet of "pied wind-flowers, and violets," of "faint oxlips," and "tender blue-bells, at whose birth the earth scarce heaved"—of "wild roses" and the rest of Flora's sweetest children,—not "Ariel to Miranda," in which some of the sweetest operations of the Soul of the Universe are conjured up in the imagination in a strain as purely spiritual, and to deep-souled sage, or to deep-hearted maiden and youth, as delicious as ever flowed from the lips of that "quaint spirit," the "delicate Ariel" of the "still-vexed Bermoothes" himself,—not in "The Cloud," that "gossamer-spun web" of the most brilliant, airy, fantastic, and most delightful fancies —nay, not in "The Skylark," that strain which wells up from the depths of the poet's heart like a pellucid fount whose waters bubble, and flash, and sparkle in the light of the noonday sun, is there a spell so subtle or powerful as that which lurks in the feeling, the sentiment, and the melody of some of his briefest and tiniest lyrics. Read the pieces beginning with the lines, "That time is dead for ever, child," "When passion's trance is overpast," "The keen stars were twinkling," "I arise from dreams of thee," "He came like a dream in the dawn of life," "The warm sun is failing," "My faint spirit was sitting in the light," "From the rivers and highlands," "Away! the moor is dark beneath the moon":—read any of the songs beginning with these lines—and many others nearly as fine could be added to the list—and you read what goes direct to the heart and remains there. I have repeatedly alluded to the rarity of Shelley's music. Each of the above-named pieces has a melody of its own, and that melody in each case is a perfect reflex in sound of the feeling and sentiment which lies at the root of the lyric. Not so much as a metrical harmonist, however, as a metrical melodist, as Mr. Devey finely suggests, doth Shelley's rare excellence as a singer rest. In metrical harmonies he has been equalled and surpassed, but in pure melody—when we consider the number, the originality, the vast variety and utter perfection of his word-tunes, we are forced to place him at the head of all the verse-melodists who have left any specimens of their gift on record. Shelley is, in verity, the king of verse melodists. That title at least must be conceded to him, though in sheer quality of melody and other essentials of lyric song he has been at least equalled, if not excelled, by Shakespeare. Shelley, to whom the lyric was a channel through which he would pour out his own richest and most precious personal feelings, has indeed left a number of pieces characterised by a beauty of sentiment which is only equalled by two or three of the tiny songlets of Shakespeare, to whom, on the other hand, the lyric was merely the medium through which he would utter the supposed feeling or fancy of the moment of others, but against this must be set an airiness and spontaneity of utterance in all cases unmatched even by Shelley, while the wonderful dramatic propriety of expression displayed in those utterances is in itself a quality of the highest and most supreme value in song—and one too, by the way, to which Shelley can lay little or no claim. Indeed, in this latter quality I know of no poet who has made the least approach to Shakespeare, except Burns, and that poet too is also notable for his spontaneity, airiness, and melody; though in the second and last respect he is far below Shelley, as in spontaniety and all other songessentials he is below Shakespeare; and so on the score of sheer quality alone must be put aside in a consideration as to whom shall be assigned the highest honour in lyric song. But if, on the other hand, fertility of faculty and quantity of lyric product, that product comprising as it does a series of pictures typical of a vaster number of the various phases of human passion and character than is to be found in any other songsters be considered—and many eminent critics appear to think that these ought on such an occasion to be considered,--then it would be a question if Burns had not as just a claim as either Shelley or Shakespeare themselves to the contested laurel. This is a question on which critics, in all likelihood, will at all times differ, and on which the mass of readers will exercise their own judgment, whatever critics may think; but of this we may rest assured, whatever the prevailing opinion as to the relative position as lyrists these bards ought to occupy, that just as the intrinsic value of their songs will remain untouched by such opinion, so just will that intrinsic value cause these songs through all time to be cherished as among the brightest, the purest, the richest, the rarest, and if in size the smallest, in quality the most precious of all the precious jewels that sparkle in the crown of British song. Then to think of some of the larger jewels that were placed in that crown by the same three bards ! Of the addresses to "The Mouse," to "The Deil," "The Mare Maggie," and the "Tam O'Shanter" of the one;

the "Epipsychidion," the "Prometheus," the "Julian and Maddalo," and the "Cenci" of the other; the "Tempest," the "Macbeth," the "Romeo and Juliet," and of "Hamlet" and many more of the highest value of the third! and then, as a compliment to our national vanity to think that all these three, among others, were of British blood! But I must conclude, and shall only add that the lyrics, the lesser poems, and the more perfect of the narrative poems of Shelley are contained in our present volume; and that it is in view on some fitting future occasion to also issue the dramas in the same series.

JOSEPH SKIPSEY.

August 1884.

Shelley's Poetical Works.

ALASTOR; OR, THE SPIRIT OF SOLITUDE.

PREFACE.

THE poem entitled *Alastor* may be considered as allegorical of one of the most interesting situations of the human mind. It represents a youth of uncorrupted feelings and adventurous genius, led forth, by an imagination inflamed and purified through familiarity with all that is excellent and majestic, to the contemplation of the universe. He drinks deep of the fountains of knowledge, and is still insatiate. The magnificence and beauty of the external world sinks profoundly into the frame of his conceptions, and affords to their modifications a variety not to be exhausted. So long as it is possible for his desires to point towards objects thus infinite and unmeasured, he is joyous and tranquil and self-possessed. But the period arrives when these objects cease to suffice. His mind is at length suddenly awakened, and thirsts for intercourse with an intelligence similar to itself. He images to himself the Being whom he loves. Conversant with speculations of the sublimest and most perfect natures, the vision in which he embodies his own imaginations unites all of wonderful or wise or beautiful which the poet, the philosopher, or the lover, could depicture. The intellectual faculties, the imagination, the functions of sense, have their respective requisitions on the sympathy of corresponding powers in other human beings. The Poet is represented as uniting these requisitions and attaching them to a single image. He seeks in vain for a prototype of his conception. Blasted by his disappointment, he descends to an untimely grave.

The picture is not barren of instruction to actual men. The Poet's self-centred seclusion was avenged by the Furies of an irresistible passion pursuing him to speedy ruin. But that power which strikes the luminaries of the world with sudden darkness and extinction, by awakening them to too exquisite a perception of its influences, dooms to a slow and poisonous decay those meaner spirits that dare to abjure its dominion. Their destiny is more abject and inglorious, as their delinquency is more contemptible and pernicious. They who, deluded by no generous error, instigated by no sacred thirst of doubtful knowledge, duped by no illustrious superstition, loving nothing on this earth, and cherishing no hopes beyond, yet keep aloof from sympathies with their kind, rejoicing neither in human joy nor mourning with human grief; these, and such as they, have their apportioned curse. They languish, because none feel with them their common nature. They are morally dead. They are neither friends, nor lovers, nor fathers, nor citizens of the world, nor benefactors of their country. Among those who attempt to exist without human sympathy, the pure and tender-hearted perish, through the intensity and passion of their search after its communities when the vacancy of their spirit suddenly makes itself felt. All else, selfish, blind, and torpid, are those unforseeing multitudes who constitute, together with their own, the lasting misery and loneliness of the world. Those who love not their fellow-beings live unfruitful lives, and prepare for their old age a miserable grave.

EARTH, Ocean, Air, beloved brotherhood!
   If our great Mother has imbued my soul
With aught of natural piety to feel
Your love, and recompense the boon with mine;
If dewy morn, and odorous noon, and even,
With sunset and its gorgeous ministers,
And solemn midnight's tingling silentness;

If Autumn's hollow sighs in the sere wood,
And Winter robing with pure snow and crowns
Of starry ice the grey grass and bare boughs—
If Springs voluptuous pantings when she breathes
Her first sweet kisses—have been dear to me ;
If no bright bird, insect, or gentle beast,
I consciously have injured, but still loved
And cherished these my kindred—then forgive
This boast, belovèd brethren, and withdraw
No portion of your wonted favour now !

Mother of this unfathomable world,
Favour my solemn song ! for I have loved
Thee ever, and thee only ; I have watched
Thy shadow, and the darkness of thy steps,
And my heart ever gazes on the depth
Of thy deep mysteries. I have made my bed
In charnels and on coffins, where black Death
Keeps record of the trophies won from thee ;
Hoping to still these obstinate questionings
Of thee and thine by forcing some lone ghost,
Thy messenger, to render up the tale
Of what we are. In lone and silent hours,
When night makes a weird sound of its own stillness,
Like an inspired and desperate alchemist
Staking his very life on some dark hope,
Have I mixed awful talk and asking looks
With my most innocent love ; until strange tears,
Uniting with those breathless kisses, made
Such magic as compels the charmèd night
To render up thy charge. And, though ne'er yet
Thou hast unveiled thy inmost sanctuary,
Enough from incommunicable dream,
And twilight phantasms, and deep noonday thought,

Has shone within me, that serenely now
And moveless (as a long forgotten lyre
Suspended in the solitary dome
Of some mysterious and deserted fane)
I wait thy breath, Great Parent; that my strain
May modulate with murmurs of the air,
And motions of the forests and the sea,
And voice of living beings, and woven hymns
Of night and day, and the deep heart of man.

There was a Poet whose untimely tomb
No human hand with pious reverence reared,
But the charmed eddies of autumnal winds
Built o'er his mouldering bones a pyramid
Of mouldering leaves in the waste wilderness.
A lovely youth, no mourning maiden decked
With weeping flowers or votive cypress wreath
The lone couch of his everlasting sleep:
Gentle, and brave, and generous, no lorn bard
Breathed o'er his dark fate one melodious sigh:
He lived, he died, he sang, in solitude.
Strangers have wept to hear his passionate notes;
And virgins, as unknown he passed, have pined
And wasted for fond love of his wild eyes.
The fire of those soft orbs has ceased to burn,
And silence, too enamoured of that voice,
Locks its mute music in her rugged cell.

By solemn vision and bright silver dream
His infancy was nurtured. Every sight
And sound from the vast earth and ambient air
Sent to his heart its choicest impulses.
The fountains of divine philosophy
Fled not his thirsting lips: and all of great

Or good or lovely which the sacred past
In truth or fable consecrates he felt
And knew. When early youth had passed, he left
His cold fireside and alienated home,
To seek strange truths in undiscovered lands.
Many a wild waste and tangled wilderness
Has lured his fearless steps ; and he has bought
With his sweet voice and eyes, from savage men,
His rest and food. Nature's most secret steps
He like her shadow has pursued, where'er
The red volcano over-canopies
Its fields of snow and pinnacles of ice
With burning smoke ; or where bitumen lakes
On black bare pointed islets ever beat
With sluggish surge ; or where the secret caves,
Rugged and dark, winding among the springs
Of fire and poison inaccessible
To avarice or pride, their starry domes
Of diamond and of gold expand above
Numberless and immeasurable halls,
Frequent with crystal column, and clear shrines
Of pearl, and thrones radiant with chrysolite.
Nor had that scene of ampler majesty
Than gems or gold, the varying roof of heaven
And the green earth, lost in his heart its claims
To love and wonder. He would linger long
In lonesome vales, making the wild his home ;
Until the doves and squirrels would partake
From his innocuous hand his bloodless food,
Lured by the gentle meaning of his looks—
And the wild antelope, that starts whene'er
The dry leaf rustles in the brake, suspend
Her timid steps, to gaze upon a form
More graceful than her own.

                              His wandering step,
Obedient to high thoughts, has visited
The awful ruins of the days of old:
Athens, and Tyre, and Balbec, and the waste
Where stood Jerusalem, the fallen towers
Of Babylon, the eternal pyramids,
Memphis and Thebes, and whatsoe'er of strange,
Sculptured on alabaster obelisk,
Or jasper tomb, or mutilated sphinx,
Dark Ethopia in her desert hills
Conceals.   Among the ruined temples there,
Stupendous columns, and wild images
Of more than man, where marble dæmons watch
The zodiac's brazen mystery, and dead men
Hang their mute thoughts on the mute walls around,
He lingered, poring on memorials
Of the world's youth; through the long burning day,
Gazed on those speechless shapes; nor, when the moon
Filled the mysterious halls with floating shades,
Suspended he that task, but ever gazed
And gazed, till meaning on his vacant mind
Flashed like strong inspiration, and he saw
The thrilling secrets of the birth of time.

Meanwhile an Arab maiden brought his food,
Her daily portion, from her father's tent,
And spread her matting for his couch, and stole
From duties and repose to tend his steps:
Enamoured, yet not daring for deep awe
To speak her love—and watched his nightly sleep,
Sleepless herself, to gaze upon his lips
Parted in slumber, whence the regular breath
Of innocent dreams arose.   Then, when red morn
Made paler the pale moon, to her cold home,
Wildered, and wan, and panting, she returned.

The Poet, wandering on, through Arabie,
And Persia, and the wild Carmanian waste,
And o'er the aerial mountains which pour down
Indus and Oxus from their icy caves,
In joy and exultation held his way;
Till in the vale of Cachmire, far within
Its loneliest dell, where odorous plants entwine
Beneath the hollow rocks a natural bower,
Beside a sparkling rivulet he stretched
His languid limbs. A vision on his sleep
There came, a dream of hopes that never yet
Had flushed his cheek. He dreamed a veilèd maid
Sate near him, talking in low solemn tones.
Her voice was like the voice of his own soul
Heard in the calm of thought; its music long,
Like woven sounds of streams and breezes, held
His inmost sense suspended in its web
Of many-coloured woof and shifting hues.
Knowledge, and truth, and virtue were her theme,
And lofty hopes of divine liberty,
Thoughts the most dear to him, and poesy,
Himself a poet. Soon the solemn mood
Of her pure mind kindled through all her frame
A permeating fire. Wild numbers then
She raised, with voice stifled in tremulous sobs
Subdued by its own pathos: her fair hands
Were bare alone, sweeping from some strange harp
Strange symphony, and in their branching veins
The eloquent blood told an ineffable tale.
The beating of her heart was heard to fill
The pauses of her music, and her breath
Tumultuously accorded with those fits
Of intermitted song. Sudden she rose,
As if her heart impatiently endured

Its bursting burthen. At the sound he turned,
And saw, by the warm light of their own life,
Her glowing limbs beneath the sinuous veil
Of woven wind ; her outspread arms now bare,
Her dark locks floating in the breath of night,
Her beamy bending eyes, her parted lips
Outstretched, and pale, and quivering eagerly.
His strong heart sank and sickened with excess
Of love. He reared his shuddering limbs, and quelled
His gasping breath, and spread his arms to meet
Her panting bosom—she drew back awhile ;
Then, yielding to the irresistible joy,
With frantic gesture and short breathless cry
Folded his frame in her dissolving arms.
Now blackness veiled his dizzy eyes, and night
Involved and swallowed up the vision ; sleep,
Like a dark flood suspended in its course,
Rolled back its impulse on his vacant brain

Roused by the shock, he started from his trance,
The cold white light of morning, the blue moon,
Low in the west, the clear and garish hills,
The distinct valley and the vacant woods,
Spread round him where he stood. Whither have fled
The hues of heaven that canopied his bower
Of yesternight ? the sounds that soothed his sleep,
The mystery and the majesty of earth,
The joy, the exultation ! His wan eyes
Gaze on the empty scene as vacantly
As ocean's moon looks on the moon in heaven.
The Spirit of sweet Human Love has sent
A vision to the sleep of him who spurned
Her choicest gifts. He eagerly pursues
Beyond the realms of dream that fleeting shade ;

He overleaps the bounds.   Alas ! alas !
Were limbs, and breath, and being intertwined
Thus treacherously ?   Lost, lost, for ever lost
In the wide pathless desert of dim Sleep,
That beautiful shape !   Does the dark gate of Death
Conduct to thy mysterious paradise,
O Sleep ?   Does the bright arch of rainbow clouds,
And pendent mountains seen in the calm lake,
Lead only to a black and watery depth—
While Death's blue vault with loathliest vapours hung,
Where every shade which the foul grave exhales
Hides its dead eye from the detested day,
Conducts, O Sleep, to thy delightful realms ?
This doubt with sudden tide flowed on his heart :
The insatiate hope which it awakened stung
His brain even like despair.
       While daylight held
The sky, the Poet kept mute conference
With his still soul.   At night the passion came,
Like the fierce fiend of a distempered dream,
And shook him from his rest, and led him forth
Into the darkness.—As an eagle, grasped
In folds of the green serpent, feels her breast
Burn with the poison, and precipitates,
Through night and day, tempest, and calm, and cloud,
Frantic with dizzying anguish, her blind flight
O'er the wide aëry wilderness : thus, driven
By the bright shadow of that lovely dream,
Beneath the cold glare of the desolate night,
Through tangled swamps and deep precipitous dells,
Startling with careless step the moonlight snake,
He fled.   Red morning dawned upon his flight,
Shedding the mockery of its vital hues
Upon his cheek of death.   He wandered on

Till vast Aornos, seen from Petra's steep,
Hung o'er the low horizon like a cloud ;
Through Balk, and where the desolated tombs
Of Parthian kings scatter to every wind
Their wasting dust, wildly he wandered on,
Day after day, a weary waste of hours,
Bearing within his life the brooding care
That ever fed on its decaying flame.
And now his limbs were lean ; his scattered hair,
Sered by the autumn of strange suffering,
Sung dirges in the wind ; his listless hand
Hung like dead bone within its withered skin ;
Life, and the lustre that consumed it, shone,
As in a furnace burning secretly
From his dark eyes alone.   The cottagers,
Who ministered with human charity
His human wants, beheld with wondering awe
Their fleeting visitant.   The mountaineer,
Encountering on some dizzy precipice
That spectral form, deemed that the Spirit of Wind,
With lightning eyes, and eager breath, and feet
Disturbing not the drifted snow, had paused
In his career.   The infant would conceal
His troubled visage in his mother's robe
In terror at the glare of those wild eyes,
To remember their strange light in many a dream
Of after times.   But youthful maidens, taught
By nature, would interpret half the woe
That wasted him, would call him with false names
Brother, and friend, would press his pallid hand
At parting, and watch, dim through tears, the path
Of his departure from their father's door.

At length upon the lone Chorasmian shore

He paused, a wide and melancholy waste
Of putrid marshes. A strong impulse urged
His steps to the sea-shore. A swan was there,
Beside a sluggish stream among the reeds.
It rose as he approached, and with strong wings
Scaling the upward sky, bent its bright course
High over the immeasurable main.
His eyes pursued its flight—"Thou hast a home,
Beautiful bird ! thou voyagest to thine home,
Where thy sweet mate will twine her downy neck
With thine, and welcome thy return with eyes
Bright in the lustre of their own fond joy.
And what am I that I should linger here,
With voice far sweeter than thy dying notes,
Spirit more vast than thine, frame more attuned
To beauty, wasting these surpassing powers
In the deaf air, to the blind earth, and heaven
That echoes not my thoughts ?" A gloomy smile
Of desperate hope wrinkled his quivering lips.
For Sleep, he knew, kept most relentlessly
Its precious charge ; and silent Death exposed,
Faithless perhaps as Sleep, a shadowy lure,
With doubtful smile mocking its own strange charms.

Startled by his own thoughts, he looked around :
There was no fair fiend near him, not a sight
Or sound of awe but in his own deep mind.
A little shallop floating near the shore
Caught the impatient wandering of his gaze.
It had been long abandoned, for its sides
Gaped wide with many a rift, and its frail joints
Swayed with the undulations of the tide.
A restless impulse urged him to embark,
And meet lone Death on the drear ocean's waste ;

For well he knew that mighty shadow loves
The slimy caverns of the populous deep.

The day was fair and sunny: sea and sky
Drank its inspiring radiance, and the wind
Swept strongly from the shore, blackening the waves.
Following his eager soul, the wanderer
Leapt in the boat; he spread his cloak aloft
On the bare mast, and took his lonely seat,
And felt the boat speed o'er the tranquil sea
Like a torn cloud before the hurricane.

As one that in a silver vision floats
Obedient to the sweep of odorous winds
Upon resplendent clouds, so rapidly
Along the dark and ruffled waters fled
The straining boat. A whirlwind swept it on,
With fierce gusts and precipitating force,
Through the white ridges of the chafed sea.
The waves arose. Higher and higher still
Their fierce necks writhed beneath the tempest's
    scourge,
Like serpents struggling in a vulture's grasp.
Calm, and rejoicing in the fearful war
Of wave running on wave, and blast on blast
Descending, and black flood on whirlpool driven
With dark obliterating course, he sate:
As if their genii were the ministers
Appointed to conduct him to the light
Of those beloved eyes, the Poet sate
Holding the steady helm. Evening came on;
The beams of sunset hung their rainbow hues
High 'mid the shifting domes of sheeted spray
That canopied his path o'er the waste deep;

Twilight, ascending slowly from the east,
Entwined in duskier wreaths her braided locks
O'er the fair front and radiant eyes of Day ;
Night followed, clad with stars. On every side
More horribly the multitudinous streams
Of ocean's mountainous waste to mutual war
Rushed in dark tumult thundering, as to mock
The calm and spangled sky. The little boat
Still fled before the storm ; still fled, like foam
Down the steep cataract of a wintry river ;
Now pausing on the edge of the riven wave :
Now leaving far behind the bursting mass,
That fell, convulsing ocean—safely fled—
As if that frail and wasted human form
Had been an elemental god.
       At midnight
The moon arose : and lo ! the ethereal cliffs
Of Caucasus, whose icy summits shone
Among the stars like sunlight, and around
Whose caverned base the whirlpools and the waves,
Bursting and eddying irresistibly,
Rage and resound for ever.—Who shall save ?—
The boat fled on—the boiling torrent drove—
The crags closed round with black and jagged arms,
The shattered mountain overhung the sea ;
And faster still, beyond all human speed,
Suspended on the sweep of the smooth wave,
The little boat was driven. A cavern there
Yawned, and amid its slant and winding depths
Engulfed the rushing sea. The boat fled on
With unrelaxing speed. "Vision and Love !"
The Poet cried aloud, " I have beheld
The path of thy departure. Sleep and Death
Shall not divide us long."

                        The boat pursued
The windings of the cavern.   Daylight shone
At length upon that gloomy river's flow.
Now, where the fiercest war among the waves
Is calm, on the unfathomable stream
The boat moved slowly.   Where the mountain, riven,
Exposed those black depths to the azure sky,
Ere yet the flood's enormous volume fell
Even to the base of Caucasus with sound
That shook the everlasting rocks, the mass
Filled with one whirlpool all that ample chasm ;
Stair above stair the eddying waters rose,
Circling immeasurably fast, and laved
With alternating dash the gnarled roots
Of mighty trees that stretched their giant arms
In darkness over it.   I' the midst was left,
Reflecting yet distorting every cloud,
A pool of treacherous and tremendous calm.
Seized by the sway of the ascending stream,
With dizzy swiftness, round, and round, and round,
Ridge after ridge the straining boat arose ;
Till on the verge of the extremest curve,
Where through an opening of the rocky bank
The waters overflow, and a smooth spot
Of glassy quiet 'mid those battling tides
Is left, the boat paused shuddering.   Shall it sink
Down the abyss ? shall the reverting stress
Of that resistless gulf embosom it ?
Now shall it fall ?—A wandering stream of wind,
Breathed from the west, has caught the expanded
    sail ;
And lo ! with gentle motion, between banks
Of mossy slope, and on a placid stream,
Beneath a woven grove, it sails ; and, hark !

The ghastly torrent mingles its far roar
With the breeze murmuring in the musical woods.
Where the embowering trees recede, and leave
A little space of green expanse, the cove
Is closed by meeting banks, whose yellow flowers
For ever gaze on their own drooping eyes
Reflected in the crystal calm. The wave
Of the boat's motion marred their pensive task,
Which nought but vagrant bird, or wanton wind,
Or falling spear-grass, or their own decay,
Had e'er disturbed before. The Poet longed
To deck with their bright hues his withered hair;
But on his heart its solitude returned,
And he forbore. Not the strong impulse hid
In those flushed cheeks, bent eyes, and shadowy frame,
Had yet performed its ministry: it hung
Upon his life, as lightning in a cloud
Gleams, hovering ere it vanish, ere the floods
Of night close over it.
     The noonday sun
Now shone upon the forest, one vast mass
Of mingling shade, whose brown magnificence
A narrow vale embosoms. There, huge caves,
Scooped in the dark base of those aëry rocks,
Mocking its moans respond and roar for ever.
The meeting boughs and implicated leaves
Wove twilight o'er the Poet's path, as, led
By love, or dream, or god, or mightier Death,
He sought in Nature's dearest haunt some bank,
Her cradle, and his sepulchre. More dark
And dark the shades accumulate. The oak,
Expanding its immense and knotty arms,
Embraces the light beech. The pyramids
Of the tall cedar, overarching, frame

Most solemn domes within ; and far below,
Like clouds suspended in an emerald sky,
The ash and the acacia floating hang,
Tremulous and pale.   Like restless serpents clothed
In rainbow and in fire, the parasites,
Starred with ten thousand blossoms, flow around
The grey trunks ; and, as gamesome infants' eyes,
With gentle meanings and most innocent wiles,
Fold their beams round the hearts of those that love,
These twine their tendrils with the wedded boughs,
Uniting their close union ; the woven leaves
Make network of the dark-blue light of day
And the night's noontide clearness, mutable
As shapes in the weird clouds.   Soft mossy lawns
Beneath these canopies extend their swells,
Fragrant with perfumed herbs, and eyed with blooms
Minute yet beautiful.   One darkest glen
Sends from its woods of musk-rose twined with jasmine
A soul-dissolving odour, to invite
To some more lovely mystery.   Through the dell,
Silence and Twilight here, twin sisters, keep
Their noonday watch, and sail among the shades
Like vaporous shapes half-seen.   Beyond, a well,
Dark, gleaming, and of most translucent wave,
Images all the woven boughs above,
And each depending leaf, and every speck
Of azure sky darting between their chasms ;
Nor aught else in the liquid mirror laves
Its portraiture, but some inconstant star
Between one foliaged lattice twinkling fair,
Or painted bird sleeping beneath the moon,
Or gorgeous insect floating motionless,
Unconscious of the day, ere yet his wings
Have spread their glories to the gaze of noon.

ALASTOR.

Hither the Poet came. His eyes beheld
Their own wan light through the reflected lines
Of his thin hair, distinct in the dark depth
Of that still fountain ; as the human heart,
Gazing in dreams over the gloomy grave,
Sees its own treacherous likeness there. He heard
The motion of the leaves ; the grass that sprung
Startled, and glanced, and trembled, even to feel
An unaccustomed presence : and the sound
Of the sweet brook that from the secret springs
Of that dark fountain rose. A Spirit seemed
To stand beside him—clothed in no bright robes
Of shadowy silver or enshrining light
Borrowed from aught the visible world affords
Of grace, or majesty, or mystery ;
But—undulating woods, and silent well,
And rippling rivulet, and evening gloom
Now deepening the dark shades, for speech assuming—
Held commune with him, as if he and it
Were all that was. Only—when his regard
Was raised by intense pensiveness—two eyes,
Two starry eyes, hung in the gloom of thought,
And seemed with their serene and azure smiles
To beckon him. Obedient to the light
That shone within his soul, he went, pursuing
The windings of the dell. The rivulet,
Wanton and wild, through many a green ravine
Beneath the forest flowed. Sometimes it fell
Among the moss, with hollow harmony
Dark and profound. Now on the polished stones
It danced : like childhood, laughing as it went :
Then, through the plain in tranquil wanderings crept,
Reflecting every herb and drooping bud

* D

That overhang its quietness.—"O stream,
Whose source is inaccessibly profound,
Whither do thy mysterious waters tend?
Thou imagest my life. Thy darksome stillness,
Thy dazzling waves, thy loud and hollow gulfs,
Thy searchless fountain and invisible course,
Have each their type in me. And the wide sky
And measureless ocean may declare as soon
What oozy cavern or what wandering cloud
Contains thy waters as the universe
Tell where these living thoughts reside, when,
    stretched
Upon thy flowers, my bloodless limbs shall waste
I' the passing wind!"
                      Beside the grassy shore
Of the small stream he went; he did impress
On the green moss his tremulous step, that caught
Strong shuddering from his burning limbs. As one
Roused by some joyous madness from the couch
Of fever, he did move; yet not (like him)
Forgetful of the grave, where, when the flame
Of his frail exultation shall be spent,
He must descend. With rapid steps he went
Beneath the shade of trees, beside the flow
Of the wild babbling rivulet; and now
The forest's solemn canopies were changed
For the uniform and lightsome evening sky.
Grey rocks did peep from the spare moss, and stemmed
The struggling brook; tall spires of windlestrae
Threw their thin shadows down the rugged slope;
And nought but gnarled roots of ancient pines,
Branchless and blasted, clenched with grasping roots
The unwilling soil. A gradual change was here,
Yet ghastly. For, as fast years flow away,

The smooth brow gathers, and the hair grows thin
And white, and, where irradiate dewy eyes
Had shone, gleam stony orbs ; so from his steps
Bright flowers departed, and the beautiful shade
Of the green groves, with all their odorous winds
And musical motions. Calm he still pursued
The stream, that with a larger volume now
Rolled through the labyrinthine dell, and there
Fretted a path through its descending curves
With its wintry speed. On every side now rose
Rocks which in unimaginable forms
Lifted their black and barren pinnacles
In the light of evening, and its precipice,
Obscuring the ravine, disclosed above,
'Mid toppling stones, black gulfs, and yawning caves
Whose windings gave ten thousand various tongues
To the loud stream. Lo ! where the pass expands
Its stony jaws, the abrupt mountain breaks,
And seems with its accumulated crags
To overhang the world : for wide expand,
Beneath the wan stars and descending moon,
Islanded seas, blue mountains, mighty streams,
Dim tracks and vast robed in the lustrous gloom
Of leaden-coloured even, and fiery hills
Mingling their flames with twilight on the verge
Of the remote horizon. The near scene,
In naked and severe simplicity,
Made contrast with the universe. A pine,
Rock-rooted, stretched athwart the vacancy
Its swinging boughs, to each inconstant blast
Yielding one only response at each pause,
In most familiar cadence—with the howl,
The thunder, and the hiss, of homeless streams,
Mingling its solemn song ; whilst the broad river,

Foaming and hurrying o'er its rugged path,
Fell into that immeasurable void,
Scattering its waters to the passing winds.

Yet the grey precipice and solemn pine
And torrent were not all—one silent nook
Was there. Even on the edge of that vast mountain,
Upheld by knotty roots and fallen rocks,
It overlooked in its serenity
The dark earth and the bending vault of stars.
It was a tranquil spot, that seemed to smile
Even in the lap of horror. Ivy clasped
The fissured stones with its entwining arms,
And did embower, with leaves forever green
And berries dark, the smooth and even space
Of its inviolated floor; and here
The children of the autumnal whirlwind bore
In wanton sport those bright leaves whose decay—
Red, yellow, or ethereally pale—
Rivals the pride of summer. 'Tis the haunt
Of every gentle wind whose breath can teach
The wilds to love tranquillity. One step,
One human step alone, has ever broken
The stillness of its solitude—one voice
Alone inspired its echoes;—even that voice
Which hither came, floating among the winds,
And led the loveliest among human forms
To make their wild haunts the depository
Of all the grace and beauty that endued
Its motions, render up its majesty,
Scatter its music on the unfeeling storm,
And to the damp leaves and blue cavern mould,
Nurses of rainbow flowers and branching moss,
Commit the colours of that varying cheek,

That snowy breast, those dark and drooping eyes.
The dim and hornèd moon hung low, and poured
A sea of lustre on the horizon's verge
That overflowed its mountains. Yellow mist
Filled the unbounded atmosphere, and drank
Wan moonlight even to fulness: not a star
Shone, not a sound was heard; the very Winds,
Danger's grim playmates, on that precipice
Slept, clasped in his embrace.—O storm of Death,
Whose sightless speed divides this sullen night!
And thou, colossal Skeleton, that, still
Guiding its irresistible career,
In thy devastating omnipotence,
Art king of this frail world! from the red field
Of slaughter, from the reeking hospital,
The patriot's sacred couch, the snowy bed
Of innocence, the scaffold and the throne,
A mighty voice invokes thee! Ruin calls
His brother Death! A rare and regal prey
He hath prepared, prowling around the world;
Glutted with which, thou mayst repose, and men
Go to their graves like flowers or creeping worms,
Nor ever more offer at thy dark shrine
The unheeded tribute of a broken heart.

When on the threshold of the green recess
The wanderer's footsteps fell, he knew that death
Was on him. Yet a little, ere it fled,
Did he resign his high and holy soul
To images of the majestic past,
That paused within his passive being now,
Like winds that bear sweet music when they breathe
Through some dim latticed chamber. He did place
His pale lean hand upon the rugged trunk

Of the old pine. Upon an ivied stone
Reclined his languid head, his limbs did rest,
Diffused and motionless, on the smooth brink
Of that obscurest chasm—and thus he lay,
Surrendering to their final impulses
The hovering powers of life. Hope and despair,
The torturers, slept: no mortal pain or fear
Marred his repose; the influxes of sense,
And his own being unalloyed by pain,
Yet feebler and more feeble, calmly fed
The stream of thought, till he lay breathing there
At peace, and faintly smiling. His last sight
Was the great moon, which o'er the western line
Of the wide world her mighty horn suspended,
With whose dun beams inwoven darkness seemed
To mingle. Now upon the jaggèd hills
It rests; and still, as the divided frame
Of the vast meteor sunk, the Poet's blood,
That ever beat in mystic sympathy
With nature's ebb and flow, grew feebler still.
And, when two lessening points of light alone
Gleamed through the darkness, the alternate gasp
Of his faint respiration scarce did stir
The stagnate night—till the minutest ray
Was quenched, the pulse yet lingered in his heart.
It paused—it fluttered. But, when heaven remained
Utterly black, the murky shades involved
An image silent, cold, and motionless,
As their own voiceless earth and vacant air.
Even as a vapour, fed with golden beams
That ministered on sunlight ere the west
Eclipses it, was now that wondrous frame—
No sense, no motion, no divinity—
A fragile lute, on whose harmonious strings

The breath of heaven did wander—a bright stream
Once fed with many-voicèd waves (a dream
Of youth which night and time have quenched for
    ever),
Still, dark, and dry, and unremembered now.

Oh for Medea's wondrous alchemy,
Which, wheresoe'er it fell, made the earth gleam
With bright flowers, and the wintry boughs exhale
From vernal blooms fresh fragrance ! Oh that God,
Profuse of poisons, would concede the chalice
Which but one living man has drained, who now,
Vessel of deathless wrath, a slave that feels
No proud exemption in the blighting curse
He bears, over the world wanders for ever,
Lone as incarnate death ! Oh that the dream
Of dark magician in his visioned cave,
Raking the cinders of a crucible
For life and power even when his feeble hand
Shakes in its last decay, were the true law
Of this so lovely world !—But thou art fled,
Like some frail exhalation which the dawn
Robes in its golden beams—ah ! thou hast fled !
The brave, the gentle, and the beautiful,
The child of grace and genius ! Heartless things
Are done and said i' the world, and many worms
And beasts and men live on, and mighty earth,
From sea and mountain, city and wilderness,
In vesper low or joyous orison,
Lifts still its solemn voice : but thou art fled—
Thou canst no longer know or love the shapes
Of this phantasmal scene, who have to thee
Been purest ministers, who are, alas !
Now thou art not ! Upon those pallid lips,

So sweet even in their silence, on those eyes
That image sleep in death, upon that form
Yet safe from the worm's outrage, let no tear
Be shed—not even in thought. Nor, when those hues
Are gone, and those divinest lineaments,
Worn by the senseless wind, shall live alone
In the frail pauses of this feeble strain,
Let not high verse mourning the memory
Of that which is no more, or painting's woe,
Or sculpture, speak in feeble imagery
Their own cold powers. Art and eloquence,
And all the shows o' the world, are frail and vain
To weep a loss that turns their lights to shade.
It is a woe "too deep for tears" when all
Is reft at once, when some surpassing Spirit,
Whose light adorned the world around it, leaves
Those who remain behind, not sobs or groans,
The passionate tumult of a clinging hope—
But pale despair and cold tranquillity,
Nature's vast frame, the web of human things,
Birth and the grave, that are not as they were.

EARLY POEMS.

TO COLERIDGE.

1. OH! there are spirits in the air,
    And genii of the evening breeze,
   And gentle ghosts with eyes as fair
    As starbeams among twilight trees—
   Such lovely ministers to meet
   Oft hast thou turned from men thy lonely feet.

2. With mountain winds, and babbling springs,
    And moonlight seas, that are the voice
   Of these inexplicable things,
    Thou didst hold commune, and rejoice
   When they did answer thee. But they
   Cast like a worthless boon thy love away.

3. And thou hast sought in starry eyes
    Beams that were never meant for thine,
   Another's wealth—tame sacrifice
    To a fond faith! Still dost thou pine?
   Still dost thou hope that greeting hands,
   Voice, looks, or lips, may answer thy demands?

4. Ah! wherefore didst thou build thine hope
    On the false earth's inconstancy?
  Did thine own mind afford no scope
    Of love or moving thoughts to thee—
  That natural scenes or human smiles
  Could steal the power to wind thee in their wiles?

5. Yes, all the faithless smiles are fled
    Whose falsehood left thee broken-hearted;
  The glory of the moon is dead;
    Night's ghosts and dreams have now departed:
  Thine own soul still is true to thee,
  But changed to a foul fiend through misery.

6. This fiend, whose ghastly presence ever
    Beside thee like thy shadow hangs,
  Dream not to chase—the mad endeavour
    Would scourge thee to severer pangs.
  Be as thou art. Thy settled fate,
  Dark as it is, all change would aggravate.

STANZAS—APRIL 1814.

AWAY! the moor is dark beneath the moon,
    Rapid clouds have drunk the last pale beam
      of even:
  Away! the gathering winds will call the darkness
    soon,
And profoundest midnight shroud the serene lights of
    heaven.

STANZAS.

Pause not! the time is past! Every voices cries
"Away!"
Tempt not with one last glance thy friend's ungentle
mood:
Thy lover's eye, so glazed and cold, dares not entreat
thy stay:
Duty and dereliction guide thee back to solitude.

Away, away! to thy sad and silent home;
Pour bitter tears on its desolated hearth;
Watch the dim shades as like ghosts they go
and come,
And complicate strange webs of melancholy mirth.
The leaves of wasted autumn woods shall float around
thine head, - [thy feet:
The blooms of dewy Spring shall gleam beneath
But thy soul or this world must fade in the frost
that binds the dead,
Ere midnight's frown and morning's smile, ere thou and
peace, may meet.

The cloud shadows of midnight possess their own
repose,
For the weary winds are silent, or the moon is in the deep;
Some respite to its turbulence unresting ocean knows;
Whatever moves or toils or grieves hath its appointed
sleep. [toms flee
Thou in the grave shalt rest—yet, till the phan-
Which that house and heath and garden made dear
to thee erewhile,
Thy remembrance and repentance and deep musings are
not free
From the music of two voices, and the light of one
sweet smile.

MUTABILITY.

1. WE are as clouds that veil the midnight moon;
    How restlessly they speed and gleam and quiver,
  Streaking the darkness radiantly! yet soon
    Night closes round, and they are lost for ever:

2. Or like forgotten lyres whose dissonant strings
    Give various response to each varying blast,
  To whose frail frame no second motion brings
    One mood or modulation like the last.

3. We rest—a dream has power to poison sleep;
    We rise—one wandering thought pollutes the day;
  We feel, conceive, or reason, laugh or weep,
    Embrace fond woe, or cast our cares away.

4. It is the same!—For, be it joy or sorrow,
    The path of its departure still is free;
  Man's yesterday may ne'er be like his morrow;
    Nought may endure but Mutability.

ON DEATH.

"There is no work nor device nor knowledge nor wisdom in the grave whither thou goest."—ECCLESIASTES.

1. THE pale, the cold, and the moony smile
    Which the meteor beam of a starless night
  Sheds on a lonely and sea-girt isle
    Ere the dawning of morn's undoubted light

ON DEATH.

    Is the flame of life so fickle and wan
    That flits round our steps till their strength is gone.

2. O man ! hold thee on in courage of soul
    Through the stormy shades of thy worldly way ;
  And the billows of cloud that around thee roll
    Shall sleep in the light of a wondrous day,
  Where hell and heaven shall leave thee free
  To the universe of destiny.

3. This world is the nurse of all we know,
    This world is the mother of all we feel ;
  And the coming of death is a fearful blow
    To a brain unencompassed with nerves of steel,
  When all that we know or feel or see
  Shall pass like an unreal mystery.

4. The secret things of the grave are there
    Where all but this frame must surely be,
  Though the fine-wrought eye and the wondrous ear
    No longer will live to hear or to see
  All that is great and all that is strange
  In the boundless realm of unending change.

5. Who telleth a tale of unspeaking death ?
    Who lifteth the veil of what is to come ?
  Who painteth the shadows that are beneath
    The wide-winding caves of the peopled tomb ?
  Or uniteth the hopes of what shall be
  With the fears and the love for that which we see ?

A SUMMER-EVENING CHURCHYARD, LECHLADE, GLOUCESTERSHIRE.

1. THE wind has swept from the wide atmosphere
    Each vapour that obscured the sunset's ray,
And pallid Evening twines its beaming hair
 In duskier braids around the languid eyes of Day:
    Silence and Twilight, unbeloved of men,
    Creep hand in hand from yon obscurest glen.

2. They breathe their spells towards the departing day,
    Encompassing the earth, air, stars, and sea;
Light, sound, and motion, own the potent sway,
 Responding to the charm with its own mystery.
    The winds are still, or the dry church-tower grass
    Knows not their gentle motions as they pass.

3. Thou too, aërial pile, whose pinnacles
    Point from one shrine like pyramids of fire,
Obey'st in silence their sweet solemn spells,
 Clothing in hues of heaven thy dim and distant spire,
    Around whose lessening and invisible height
    Gather among the stars the clouds of night.

4. The dead are sleeping in their sepulchres:
    And, mouldering as they sleep, a thrilling sound,
Half sense, half thought, among the darkness stirs,
 Breathed from their wormy beds all living things around;
    And, mingling with the still night and mute sky,
    Its awful hush is felt inaudibly.

5. Thus solemnized and softened, death is mild
   And terrorless as the serenest night.
   Here could I hope, like some inquiring child
Sporting on graves, that death did hide from human
   sight
   Sweet secrets, or beside its breathless sleep
   That loveliest dreams perpetual watch did keep.

TO WORDSWORTH.

POET of Nature, thou hast wept to know
   That things depart which never may return;
Childhood and youth, friendship and love's first glow,
   Have fled like sweet dreams, leaving thee to mourn.
These common woes I feel. One loss is mine,
   Which thou too feel'st, yet I alone deplore.
Thou wert as a lone star whose light did shine
   On some frail bark in winter's midnight roar:
Thou hast like to a rock-built refuge stood
Above the blind and battling multitude:
In honoured poverty thy voice did weave
   Songs consecrate to truth and liberty.
Deserting these, 'thou leavest me to grieve,
   Thus, having been, that thou shouldst cease to be.

FEELINGS OF A REPUBLICAN ON THE FALL OF BONAPARTE.

I HATED thee, fallen Tyrant! I did groan
  To think that a most unambitious slave,
    Like thou, should dance and revel on the grave
Of Liberty. Thou mightst have built thy throne
Where it had stood even now: thou didst prefer
  A frail and bloody pomp, which Time has swept
In fragments towards oblivion. Massacre,
  For this, I prayed, would on thy sleep have crept,
Treason and Slavery, Rapine, Fear, and Lust,
  And stifled thee their minister. I know
Too late, since thou and France are in the dust,
  That Virtue owns a more eternal foe
Then Force or Fraud; old Custom, Legal Crime,
And bloody Faith, the foulest birth of Time.

LINES.

1. THE cold earth slept below;
     Above, the cold sky shone;
   And all around,
     With a chilling sound,
   From caves of ice and fields of snow
   The breath of night like death did flow
     Beneath the sinking moon.

2. The wintry hedge was black;
     The green grass was not seen;

The birds did rest
   On the bare thorn's breast,
Whose roots, beside the pathway track,
Had bound their folds o'er many a crack
   Which the frost had made between.

3. Thine eyes glowed in the glare
   Of the moon's dying light.
      As a fen-fire's beam
      On a sluggish stream
   Gleams dimly, so the moon shone there;
   And it yellowed the strings of thy tangled hair,
      That shook in the wind of night.

4. The moon made thy lips pale, beloved;
   The wind made thy bosom chill;
      The night did shed
      On thy dear head
   Its frozen dew, and thou didst lie
   Where the bitter breath of the naked sky
      Might visit thee at will.

November 1815.

POEMS WRITTEN IN 1816.

THE SUNSET.

THERE late was one within whose subtle being,
    As light and wind within some delicate cloud
That fades amid the blue noon's burning sky,
Genius and death contended. None may know
The sweetness of the joy which made his breath
Fail like the trances of the summer air,
When, with the lady of his love, who then
First knew the unreserve of mingled being,
He walked along the pathway of a field,
Which to the east a hoar wood shadowed o'er,
But to the west was open to the sky.
There now the sun had sunk; but lines of gold
Hung on the ashen clouds, and on the points
Of the far level grass and nodding flowers,
And the old dandelion's hoary beard,
And, mingled with the shades of twilight, lay
On the brown massy woods—and in the east
The broad and burning moon lingeringly rose
Between the black trunks of the crowded trees,
While the faint stars were gathering overhead.—
"Is it not strange, Isabel," said the youth,

THE SUNSET.

"I never saw the sun ! We will walk here
To-morrow ; thou shalt look on it with me."

That night the youth and lady mingled lay
In love and sleep—but when the morning came
The lady found her lover dead and cold.
Let none believe that God in mercy gave
That stroke. The lady died not nor grew wild,
But year by year lived on—in truth I think
Her gentleness and patience and sad smiles,
And that she did not die but lived to tend
Her aged father, were a kind of madness,
If madness 'tis to be unlike the world.
For but to see her were to read the tale
Woven by some subtlest bard, to make hard hearts
Dissolve away in wisdom-working grief—
Her eyelashes were torn away with tears,
Her lips and cheeks were like things dead—so pale ;
Her hands were thin, and through their wandering
   veins
And weak articulations might be seen
Day's ruddy light. The tomb of thy dead self
Which one vexed ghost inhabits, night and day,
Is all, lost child, that now remains of thee !

"Inheritor of more than earth can give,
Passionless calm and silence unreproved—
Whether the dead find—oh ! not sleep—but rest,
And are the uncomplaining things they seem,
Or live, or drop in the deep sea of Love ;
Oh ! that, like thine, mine epitaph were—Peace !"
This was the only moan she ever made.

Bishopgate, Spring 1816.

HYMN TO INTELLECTUAL BEAUTY.

1. THE awful shadow of some unseen Power
    Floats, though unseen, among us; visiting
This various world with as inconstant wing
As summer winds that creep from flower to flower.
Like moonbeams that behind some piny mountain shower,
    It visits with inconstant glance
    Each human heart and countenance;
Like hues and harmonies of evening,
    Like clouds in starlight widely spread,
    Like memory of music fled,
    Like aught that for its grace may be
Dear, and yet dearer for its mystery.

2. Spirit of BEAUTY, that dost consecrate
    With thine own hues all thou dost shine upon
Of human thought or form, where art thou gone?
Why dost thou pass away, and leave our state,
This dim vast vale of tears, vacant and desolate—
    Ask why the sunlight not for ever
    Weaves rainbows o'er yon mountain river;
Why aught should fail and fade that once is shown;
    Why fear, and dream, and death, and birth
    Cast on the daylight of this earth
    Such gloom; why man has such a scope
For love and hate, despondency and hope!

3. No voice from some sublimer world hath ever
    To sage or poet these responses given:
    Therefore the names of Demon, Ghost, and Heaven,
Remain the records of their vain endeavour;

Frail spells, whose uttered charm might not avail to sever,
    From all we hear and all we see,
    Doubt, chance, and mutability.
  Thy light alone, like mist o'er mountains driven,
    Or music by the night-wind sent
    Through strings of some still instrument,
    Or moonlight on a midnight stream,
Gives grace and truth to life's unquiet dream.

4. Love, hope, and self-esteem, like clouds depart
    And come for some uncertain moments lent.
    Man were immortal and omnipotent,
Didst thou, unknown and awful as thou art,
Keep with thy glorious train firm state within his heart.
    Thou messenger of sympathies
    That wax and wane in lovers' eyes!
  Thou that to human thought art nourishment,
    Like darkness to a dying flame!
    Depart not as thy shadow came:
    Depart not, lest the grave should be,
Like life and fear, a dark reality!

5. While yet a boy, I sought for ghosts, and sped
  Through many a listening chamber, cave, and ruin,
  And starlight wood, with fearful steps pursuing
Hopes of high talk with the departed dead.
I called on poisonous names with which our youth is fed.
    I was not heard, I saw them not;
    When musing deeply on the lot
  Of life, at that sweet time when winds are wooing
    All vital things that wake to bring
    News of birds and blossoming,
    Sudden thy shadow fell on me—
I shrieked, and clasped my hands in ecstasy!

6. I vowed that I would dedicate my powers
      To thee and thine : have I not kept the vow ?
      With beating heart and streaming eyes, even now
   I called the phantoms of a thousands hours
 Each from his voiceless grave. They have in visioned
            bowers
         Of studious zeal or love's delight
         Outwatched with me the envious night :
         They know that never joy illumed my brow,
            Unlinked with hope that thou wouldst free
         This world from its dark slavery ;
         That thou, O awful Loveliness,
 Wouldst give whate'er these words cannot express.

7. The day becomes more solemn and serene
      When noon is past ; there is a harmony
      In autumn, and a lustre in its sky,
   Which through the summer is not heard nor seen.
 As if it could not be, as if it had not been.
         Thus let thy power, which like the truth
         Of Nature on my passive youth
      Descended, to my onward life supply
         Its calm—to one who worships thee,
         And every form containing thee,
         Whom, Spirit fair, thy spells did bind
   To fear himself, and love all humankind.

MONT BLANC.

LINES WRITTEN IN THE VALE OF CHAMOUNI.

1. THE everlasting universe of Things
    Flows through the Mind, and rolls its rapid
        waves,
    Now dark — now glittering — now reflecting
        gloom—
Now lending splendour, where from secret springs
The source of human thought its tribute brings
Of waters—with a sound but half its own,
    Such as a feeble brook will oft assume
In the wild woods, among the mountains lone,
Where waterfalls around it leap for ever,
Where woods and winds contend, and a vast river
    Over its rocks ceaselessly bursts and raves.

2. Thus thou, Ravine of Arve—dark, deep Ravine—
    Thou many-coloured many-voicèd vale,
    Over whose pines, and crags, and caverns sail
Fast cloud-shadows and sunbeams; awful scene,
Where Power in likeness of the Arve comes down
From the ice-gulfs that gird his secret throne,
Bursting through these dark mountains like the flame
    Of lightning through the tempest; thou dost lie—
    Thy giant brood of pines around thee clinging,
        Children of elder time, in whose devotion
The chainless winds still come and ever came
    To drink their odours, and their mighty swinging
To hear, an old and solemn harmony;
        Thine earthly rainbows stretched across the sweep
            Of the ethereal waterfall, whose veil

Robes some unsculptured image; the strange
 sleep
    Which, when the voices of the desert fail,
Wraps all in its own deep eternity;
    Thy caverns echoing to the Arve's commotion,
A loud lone sound no other sound can tame.
    Thou art pervaded with that ceaseless motion,
Thou art the path of that unresting sound,
    Dizzy Ravine! And, when I gaze on thee,
    I seem, as in a trance sublime and strange,
    To muse on my own separate fantasy,
    My own, my human mind, which passively
    Now renders and receives fast influencings,
    Holding an unremitting interchange
With the clear universe of things around;
    One legion of wild thoughts, whose wandering wings
Now float above thy darkness, and now rest
Where that or thou art no unbidden guest,
    In the still cave of the witch Poesy—
    Seeking, among the shadows that pass by,
    Ghosts of all things that are—some shade of thee,
Some phantom, some faint image. Till the breast
From which they fled recalls them, thou art there!

3. Some say that gleams of a remoter world
    Visit the soul in sleep—that death is slumber,
    And that its shapes the busy thoughts outnumber
    Of those who wake and live. I look on high;
Has some unknown omnipotence unfurled
    The veil of life and death? Or do I lie
In dream, and does the mightier world of sleep
    Spread far around and inaccessibly
        Its circles? for the very spirit fails,
Driven like a homeless cloud from step to steep

That vanishes among the viewless gales !
Far, far above, piercing the infinite sky,
Mont Blanc appears—still, snowy, and serene.
Its subject mountains their unearthly forms
Pile around it, ice and rock ; broad vales between
Of frozen floods, unfathomable deeps,
    Blue as the overhanging heaven, that spread
And wind among the accumulated steeps ;
A desert peopled by the storms alone,
Save when the eagle brings some hunter's bone,
And the wolf tracks her there. How hideously
Its shapes are heaped around—rude, bare, and high,
Ghastly, and scared, and riven !—Is this the scene
Where the old Earthquake-dæmon taught her young
    Ruin ? were these their toys ? or did a sea
    Of fire envelop once this silent snow ?
    None can reply—all seems eternal now.
The wilderness has a mysterious tongue
    Which teaches awful doubt—or faith so mild,
    So solemn, so serene, that Man may be,
    But for such faith, with Nature reconciled.
Thou hast a voice, great Mountain, to repeal
    Large codes of fraud and woe ; not understood
    By all, but which the wise, and great, and good
Interpret, or make felt, or deeply feel.

4. The fields, the lakes, the forests, and the streams,
    Ocean, and all the living things that dwell
    Within the dædal earth, lightning and rain,
    Earthquake and fiery flood and hurricane,
The torpor of the year when feeble dreams
Visit the hidden buds, or dreamless sleep
    Holds every future leaf and flower, the bound
With which from that detested trance they leap,

The works and ways of man, their death and
    birth,
  And that of him, and all that his may be,
All things that move and breathe, with toil and
    sound
Are born and die, revolve, subside, and swell.
    Power dwells apart in its tranquillity,
Remote, serene, and inaccessible:
  And *this* the naked countenance of earth
On which I gaze, even these primæval mountains,
Teach the adverting mind. The glaciers creep,
  Like snakes that watch their prey, from their far
    fountains,
Slow rolling on ; there, many a precipice
  Frost and the sun in scorn of mortal power
Have piled—dome, pyramid, and pinnacle,
  A city of death, distinct with many a tower
And wall impregnable of beaming ice.
  Yet not a city, but a flood of ruin,
Is there, that from the boundary of the skies
  Rolls its perpetual stream ; vast pines are strewing
Its destined path, or in the mangled soil
  Branchless and shattered stand ; the rocks, drawn
    down
From yon remotest waste, have overthrown
  The limits of the dead and living world,
  Never to be reclaimed. The dwelling-place
Of insects, beasts, and birds, becomes its spoil ;
  Their food and their retreat for ever gone,
  So much of life and joy is lost. The race
Of man flies far in dread ; his work and dwelling
  Vanish like smoke before the tempest's stream,
    And their place is not known. Below, vast caves
Shine in the rushing torrents' restless gleam,

MONT BLANC.

    Which, from those secret chasms in tumult welling,
    Meet in the Vale ; and one majestic River,
    The breath and blood of distant lands, for ever
        Rolls its loud waters to the ocean waves,
    Breathes its swift vapours to the circling air.

5. Mont Blanc yet gleams on high : the power is there,
      The still and solemn power, of many sights
        And many sounds, and much of life and death.
      In the calm darkness of the moonless nights,
      In the lone glare of day, the snows descend
    Upon that Mountain ; none beholds them there,
    Nor when the flakes burn in the sinking sun,
        Or the star-beams dart through them. Winds contend
      Silently there, and heap the snow, with breath
    Rapid and strong, but silently. Its home
      The voiceless lightning in these solitudes
      Keeps innocently, and like vapour broods
      Over the snow. The secret Strength of Things,
    Which governs thought, and to the infinite dome
    Of heaven is as a law, inhabits thee.
    And what were thou and earth and stars and sea,
      If to the human mind's imaginings
    Silence and solitude were vacancy ?

23rd June 1816.

JULIAN AND MADDALO.

A CONVERSATION.

Count Maddalo is a Venetian nobleman of ancient family and of great fortune, who, without mixing much in the society of his countrymen, resides chiefly at his magnificent palace in that city. He is a person of the most consummate genius, and capable, if he would direct his energies to such an end, of becoming the redeemer of his degraded country. But it is his weakness to be proud: he derives, from a comparison of his own extraordinary mind with the dwarfish intellects that surround him, an intense apprehension of the nothingness of human life. His passions and his powers are incomparably greater than those of other men; and, instead of the latter having been employed in curbing the former, they have mutually lent each other strength. His ambition preys upon itself, for want of objects which it can consider worthy of exertion. I say that Maddalo is proud, because I can find no other word to express the concentrated and impatient feelings which consume him; but it is on his own hopes and affections only that he seems to trample, for in social life no human being can be more gentle, patient, and unassuming than Maddalo. He is cheerful, frank, and witty. His more serious conversation is a sort of intoxication: men are held by it as by a spell. He has travelled much, and there is an inexpressible charm in his relation of his adventures in different countries.

Julian is an Englishman of good family; passionately attached to those philosophical notions which assert the power of man over his own mind, and the immense improvements of which, by the extinction of certain moral superstitions, human society may yet be susceptible. Without concealing the evil in the world, he is for ever speculating how good may be made superior. He is a complete infidel, and a scoffer at all things reputed holy; and Maddalo takes a wicked pleasure in drawing out his taunts against religion. What Maddalo thinks on these matters is not exactly known. Julian, in spite of his heterodox opinions, is conjectured by his friends to possess some good qualities. How far this is possible the pious reader will determine. Julian is rather serious.

Of the Maniac I can give no information. He seems, by his own account, to have been disappointed in love. He was evidently a very cultivated and amiable person when in his right senses. His story, told at length, might be like many other stories of the same kind: the unconnected exclamations of his agony will perhaps be found a sufficient comment for the text of every heart.

"The meadows with fresh streams, the bees with thyme,
The goats with the green leaves of budding Spring,
Are saturated not—nor Love with tears."—VIRGIL'S GALLUS.

I RODE one evening with Count Maddalo
Upon the bank of land which breaks the flow
Of Adria towards Venice. A bare strand
Of hillocks heaped from ever-shifting sand,
Matted with thistles and amphibious weeds
Such as from earth's embrace the salt ooze breeds,
Is this; an uninhabited sea-side,
Which the lone fisher, when his nets are dried,
Abandons. And no other object breaks
The waste, but one dwarf tree, and some few stakes
Broken and unrepaired; and the tide makes
A narrow space of level sand thereon,
Where 'twas our wont to ride while day went down.
This ride was my delight. I love all waste
And solitary places; where we taste
The pleasure of believing what we see
Is boundless, as we wish our souls to be:
And such was this wide ocean, and this shore
More barren than its billows. And, yet more

Than all, with a remembered friend I love
To ride as then I rode—for the winds drove
The living spray along the sunny air
Into our faces; the blue heavens were bare,
Stripped to their depths by the awakening north;
And from the waves sound like delight broke forth,
Harmonising with solitude, and sent
Into our hearts aërial merriment.

So, as we rode, we talked; and the swift thought,
Winging itself with laughter, lingered not,
But flew from brain to brain. Such glee was ours,
Charged with light memories of remembered hours,
None slow enough for sadness; till we came
Homeward, which always makes the spirit tame.
This day had been cheerful, but cold; and now
The sun was sinking, and the wind also.
Our talk grew somewhat serious, as may be
Talk interrupted with such raillery
As mocks itself, because it cannot scorn
The thoughts it would extinguish—'twas forlorn,
Yet pleasing; such as once, so poets tell,
The devils held within the vales of hell,
Concerning God, freewill, and destiny.
Of all that Earth has been, or yet may be;
All that vain men imagine or believe,
Or hope can paint, or suffering can achieve,
We descanted; and I (for ever still
Is it not wise to make the best of ill?)
Argued against despondency; but pride
Made my companion take the darker side.
The sense that he was greater than his kind
Had struck, methink, his eagle spirit blind
By gazing on its own exceeding light.

Meanwhile the sun paused ere it should alight
Over the horizon of the mountains. Oh !
How beautiful is sunset, when the glow
Of heaven descends upon a land like thee,
Thou paradise of exiles, Italy,
Thy mountains, seas, and vineyards, and the towers
Of cities they encircle ! It was ours
To stand on thee, beholding it : and then,
Just where we had dismounted, the Count's men
Were waiting for us with the gondola.
As those who pause on some delightful way,
Though bent on pleasant pilgrimage, we stood
Looking upon the evening, and the flood
Which lay between the city and the shore,
Paved with the image of the sky. The hoar
And aery Alps, towards the north, appeared
Through mist—an heaven-sustaining bulwark reared
Between the east and west ; and half the sky
Was roofed with clouds of rich emblazonry,
Dark purple at the zenith, which still grew
Down the steep west into a wondrous hue
Brighter than burning gold, even to the rent
Where the swift sun yet paused in his descent
Among the many-folded hills. They were
Those famous Euganean hills, which bear,
As seen from Lido through the harbour piles,
The likeness of a clump of peaked isles.
And then, as if the earth and sea had been
Dissolved into one lake of fire, were seen
Those mountains towering, as from waves of flame,
Around the vaporous sun ; from which there came
The inmost purple spirit of light, and made
Their very peaks transparent.
                          " Ere it fade,"

Said my companion, " I will show you soon
A better station."
                    So, o'er the lagune
We glided ; and from that funereal bark
I leaned, and saw the city, and could mark
How from their many isles, in evening's gleam,
Its temples and its palaces did seem
Like fabrics of enchantment piled to heaven.
I was about to speak, when——
                              " We are even
Now at the point I meant," said Maddalo—
And bade the gondolieri cease to row.
" Look, Julian, on the west, and listen well
If you hear not a deep and heavy bell."

I looked, and saw between us and the sun
A building on an island, such an one
As age to age might add, for uses vile—
A windowless, deformed, and dreary pile ;
And on the top an open tower, where hung
A bell which in the radiance swayed and swung—
We could just hear its hoarse and iron tongue :
The broad sun sank behind it, and it tolled
In strong and black relief.
                           " What we behold
Shall be the madhouse and its belfry tower,"
Said Maddalo ; "and ever at this hour
Those who may cross the water hear that bell,
Which calls the maniacs, each one from his cell,
To vespers."
             " As much skill as need to pray
In thanks or hope for their dark lot have they
To their stern maker," I replied.
                                 " Oho !

JULIAN AND MADDALO.

You talk as in years past," said Maddalo.
"'Tis strange men change not. You were ever still
Among Christ's flock a perilous infidel,
A wolf for the meek lambs. If you can't swim,
Beware of providence!" I looked on him,
But the gay smile had faded from his eye.
"And such," he cried, "is our mortality!
And this must be the emblem and the sign
Of what should be eternal and divine;
And, like that black and dreary bell, the soul,
Hung in an heaven-illumined tower, must toll
Our thoughts and our desires to meet below
Round the rent heart, and pray—as madmen do;
For what? they know not, till the night of death,
As sunset that strange vision, severeth
Our memory from itself, and us from all
We sought and yet were baffled."
       I recall
The sense of what he said, although I mar
The force of his expressions. The broad star
Of day meanwhile had sunk behind the hill;
And the black bell became invisible;
And the red tower looked grey; and, all between,
The churches, ships, and palaces, were seen
Huddled in gloom; into the purple sea
The orange hues of heaven sunk silently.
We hardly spoke, and soon the gondola
Conveyed me to my lodging by the way.

The following morn was rainy, cold, and dim.
Ere Maddalo arose, I called on him;
And, whilst I waited, with his child I played.
A lovelier toy sweet Nature never made;
A serious, subtle, wild, yet gentle being;

Graceful without design, and unforeseeing;
With eyes—oh speak not of her eyes! which seem
Twin mirrors of Italian heaven, yet gleam
With such deep meaning as we never see
But in the human countenance. With me
She was a special favourite: I had nursed
Her fine and feeble limbs when she came first
To this bleak world; and she yet seemed to know
On second sight her ancient playfellow,
Less changed than she was by six months or so.
For, after her first shyness was worn out,
We sate there, rolling billiard balls about—
When the Count entered.   Salutations passed:
"The words you spoke last night might well have cast
A darkness on my spirit. If man be
The passive thing you say, I should not see
Much harm in the religions and old saws
(Though *I* may never own such leaden laws)
Which break a teachless nature to the yoke:
Mine is another faith." Thus much I spoke,
And, noting he replied not, added—"See
This lovely child; blithe, innocent, and free:
She spends a happy time, with little care:
While we to such sick thoughts subjected are
As came on you last night. It is our will
Which thus enchains us to permitted ill.
We might be otherwise; we might be all
We dream of—happy, high, majestical.
Where is the beauty, love, and truth, we seek,
But in our minds? And, if we were not weak,
Should we be less in deed than in desire?"

"Ay, *if* we were not weak—and we aspire,

How vainly ! to be strong," said Maddalo ;
" You talk Utopia."
                        " It remains to know,"
I then rejoined ; " and those who try may find
How strong the chains are which our spirit bind ;
Brittle perchance as straw. We are assured
Much may be conquered, much may be endured,
Of what degrades and crushes us. We know
That we have power over ourselves to do
And suffer—*what*, we know not till we try,
But something nobler than to live and die.
So taught the kings of old philosophy
Who reigned before religion made men blind ;
And those who suffer with their suffering kind
Yet feel this faith Religion."
                        "My dear friend,"
Said Maddalo, " my judgment will not bend
To your opinion, though I think you might
Make such a system refutation-tight,
As far as words go. I knew one like you,
Who to this city came some months ago,
With whom I argued in this sort—and he
Is now gone mad—and so he answered me,
Poor fellow !—But, if you would like to go,
We'll visit him, and his wild talk will show
How vain are such aspiring theories."

" I hope to prove the induction otherwise,
And that a want of that true theory still
Which seeks a soul of goodness in things ill,
Or in himself or others, has thus bowed
His being. There are some by nature proud
Who, patient in all else, demand but this—
To love and be beloved with gentleness :

And, being scorned, what wonder if they die
Some living death ? This is not destiny,
But man's own wilful ill."
                              As this I spoke,
Servants announced the gondola, and we
Through the fast-falling rain and high-wrought sea
Sailed to the island where the Madhouse stands.
We disembarked. The clap of tortured hands,
Fierce yells, and howlings, and lamentings keen,
And laughter where complaint had merrier been,
Accosted us. We climbed the oozy stairs
Into an old courtyard. I heard on high
Then fragments of most touching melody ;
But, looking up, saw not the singer there.
Through the black bars, in the tempestuous air,
I saw, like weeds on a wrecked palace growing,
Long tangled locks, flung wildly forth and flowing,
Of those who on a sudden were beguiled
Into strange silence, and looked forth and smiled,
Hearing sweet sounds. Then I:
                              "Methinks there were
A cure of these with patience and kind care,
If music can thus move. But what is he
Whom we seek here ?"
                    "Of his sad history
I know but this," said Maddalo. "He came
To Venice a dejected man, and fame
Said he was wealthy, or he had been so :
Some thought the loss of fortune wrought him woe.
But he was ever talking in such sort
As you do—but more sadly ; he seemed hurt,
Even as a man with his peculiar wrong,
To hear but of the oppression of the strong,
Or those absurd deceits (I think with you

In some respects, you know) which carry through
The excellent impostors of this earth,
When they outface detection. He had worth,
Poor fellow, but a humourist in his way."
"Alas! what drove him mad?"
        "I cannot say:
A lady came with him from France; and, when
She left him and returned, he wandered then
About yon lonely isles of desert sand,
Till he grew wild. He had no cash or land
Remaining. The police had brought him here:
Some fancy took him, and he would not bear
Removal. So I fitted up for him
Those rooms beside the sea, to please his whim;
And sent him busts, and books, and urns for flowers,
Which had adorned his life in happier hours,
And instruments of music. You may guess
A stranger could do little more, or less,
For one so gentle and unfortunate:
And those are his sweet strains which charm the weight
From madmen's chains, and make this hell appear
A heaven of sacred silence hushed to hear."

"Nay, this was kind of you—he had no claim,
As the world says."
      "None but the very same
Which I on all mankind, were I, as he,
Fallen to such deep reverse. His melody
Is interrupted now: we hear the din
Of madmen, shriek on shriek, again begin,
Let us now visit him: after this strain,
He ever communes with himself again,
And sees and hears not any."
       Having said

These words, we called the keeper, and he led
To an apartment opening on the sea.
There the poor wretch was sitting mournfully
Near a piano, his pale fingers twined
One with the other; and the ooze and wind
Rushed through an open casement, and did sway
His hair, and starred it with the brackish spray.
His head was leaning on a music-book,
And he was muttering, and his lean limbs shook.
His lips were pressed against a folded leaf,
In hue too beautiful for health; and grief
Smiled in their motions as they lay apart,
As one who wrought from his own fervid heart
The eloquence of passion. Soon he raised
His sad meek face, and eyes lustrous and glazed,
And spoke—sometimes as one who wrote, and thought
His words might move some heart that heeded not,
If sent to distant lands; and then as one
Reproaching deeds never to be undone,
With wondering self-compassion. Then his speech
Was lost in grief, and then his words came each
Unmodulated and expressionless—
But that from one jarred accent you might guess
It was despair made them so uniform.
And all the while the loud and gusty storm
Hissed through the window; and we stood behind,
Stealing his accents from the envious wind,
Unseen. I yet remember what he said
Distinctly, such impression his words made.

"Month after month," he cried, "to bear this load!
And, as a jade urged by the whip and goad,
To drag life on—which like a heavy chain
Lengthens behind with many a link of pain!

And not to speak my grief—Oh not to dare
To give a human voice to my despair !
But live, and move, and, wretched thing ! smile on,
As if I never went aside to groan—
And wear this mask of falsehood even to those
Who are most dear ; not for my own repose—
Alas ! no scorn or pain or hate could be
So heavy as that falsehood is to me—
But that I cannot bear more altered faces
Than needs must be, more changed and cold embraces,
More misery, disappointment, and mistrust,
To own me for their father. Would the dust
Were covered in upon my body now—
That the life ceased to toil within my brow !
And then these thoughts would at the last be fled :
Let us not fear such pain can vex the dead.

"What power delights to torture us ? I know
That to myself I do not wholly owe
What now I suffer, though in part I may.
Alas ! none strewed fresh flowers upon the way
Where, wandering heedlessly, I met pale Pain,
My shadow, which will leave me not again.
If I have erred, there was no joy in error,
But pain, and insult, and unrest, and terror.
I have not, as some do, bought penitence
With pleasure and a dark yet sweet offence ;
For then, if love and tenderness and truth
Had overlived hope's momentary youth,
My creed should have redeemed me from repenting.
But loathèd scorn and outrage unrelenting
Met love, excited by far other seeming,
Until the end was gained : as one from dreaming

Of sweetest peace, I woke, and found my state
Such as it is !—

              "O thou, my spirit's mate !
Who, for thou art compassionate and wise,
Wouldst pity me from thy most gentle eyes
If this sad writing thou shouldst ever see,
My secret groans must be unheard by thee ;
Thou wouldst weep tears bitter as blood, to know
Thy lost friend's incommunicable woe.
Ye few by whom my nature has been weighed
In friendship, let me not that name degrade
By placing on your hearts the secret load
Which crushes mine to dust. There is one road
To peace—and that is truth, which follow ye :
Love sometimes leads astray to misery.
Yet think not, though subdued (and I may well
Say that I am subdued), that the full hell
Within me would infect the untainted breast
Of sacred nature with its own unrest ;
As some perverted beings think to find
In scorn or hate a medicine for the mind
Which scorn or hate hath wounded—oh how vain !
The dagger heals not, but may rend again.
Believe that I am ever still the same
In creed as in resolve ; and what may tame
My heart must leave the understanding free,
Or all would sink under this agony.
Nor dream that I will join the vulgar lie,
Or with my silence sanction tyranny ;
Or seek a moment's shelter from my pain
In any madness which the world calls gain,
Ambition, or revenge, or thoughts as stern
As those which make me what I am ; or turn
To avarice or misanthropy or lust.

Heap on me soon, O grave, thy welcome dust !
Till then the dungeon may demand its prey ;
And Poverty and Shame may meet and say,
Halting beside me in the public way,
' That love-devoted youth is ours : let's sit
Beside him : he may live some six months yet.'
Or the red scaffold, as our country bends,
May ask some willing victim ; or ye, friends,
May fall under some sorrow, which this heart
Or hand may share, or vanquish, or avert.
I am prepared—in truth, with no proud joy—
To do or suffer aught ; as when, a boy,
I did devote to justice and to love
My nature, worthless now.
      " I must remove
A veil from my pent mind. 'Tis torn aside !
Oh, pallid as Death's dedicated bride,
Thou mockery which art sitting by my side,
Am I not wan like thee ? At the grave's call
I haste, invited to thy wedding-ball,
To meet the ghastly paramour for whom
Thou hast deserted me, and made the tomb
Thy bridal bed. But I beside thy feet
Will lie, and watch ye from my winding-sheet
Thus—wide awake, though dead.—Yet stay, oh, stay !
Go not so soon !—I know not what I say—
Hear but my reasons !—I am mad, I fear,
My fancy is o'erwrought.—Thou art not here ;
Pale art thou, 'tis most true——But thou art gone—
Thy work is finished ; I am left alone.

" Nay, was it I who wooed thee to this breast,
Which like a serpent thou envenomest
As in repayment of the warmth it lent !

Didst thou not seek me for thine own content ?
Did not thy love awaken mine ? I thought
That thou wert she who said, 'You kiss me not
Ever ; I fear you do not love me now.'
In truth I loved even to my overthrow
Her who would fain forget these words—but they
Cling to her mind, and cannot pass away.

"You say that I am proud ; that, when I speak,
My lip is tortured with the wrongs which break
The spirit it expresses.—Never one
Humbled himself before as I have done.
Even the instinctive worm on which we tread
Turns, though it wound not—then with prostrate head
Sinks in the dust, and writhes like me—and dies :
——No, wears a living death of agonies.
As the slow shadows of the pointed grass
Mark the eternal periods, its pangs pass,
Slow, ever-moving, making moments be
As mine seem—each an immortality !

"That you had never seen me ! never heard
My voice ! and more than all had ne'er endured
The deep pollution of my loathed embrace !
That your eyes ne'er had lied love in my face !
That, like some maniac monk, I had torn out
The nerves of manhood by their bleeding root
With mine own quivering fingers, so that ne'er
Our hearts had for a moment mingled there,
To disunite in horror ! These were not,
With thee, like some suppressed and hideous thought,
Which flits athwart our musings, but can find
No rest within a pure and gentle mind :
Thou sealedst them with many a bare broad word,

And searedst my memory o'er them—for I heard,
And can forget not—they were ministered
One after one, those curses. Mix them up
Like self-destroying poisons, in one cup ;
And they will make one blessing w' 'h thou ne'er
Didst imprecate, for on me——death !
                                    "It were
A cruel punishment for one most cruel,
If such can love, to make that love the fuel
Of the mind's hell—hate, scorn, remorse, despair.
But *me*, whose heart a stranger's tear might wear
As water-drops the sandy fountain-stone ;
Who loved and pitied all things, and could moan
For woes which others hear not, and could see
The absent with a glass of fantasy,
And near the poor and trampled sit and weep,
Following the captive to his dungeon deep ;
Me, who am as a nerve o'er which do creep
The else-unfelt oppressions of this earth,
And was to thee the flame upon thy hearth
When all beside was cold—that thou on me
Shouldst rain the plagues of blistering agony !
Such curses are, from lips once eloquent
With love's too partial praise. Let none relent
Who intend deeds too dreadful for a name,
Henceforth, if an example of the same
They seek—for thou on me lookedst so and so,
And didst speak thus and thus ! I live to show
How much men bear, and die not.
                                  "Thou wilt tell
With the grimace of hate, how horrible
It was to meet my love when thine grew less ;
Thou wilt admire how I could e'er address
Such features to love's work. This taunt, though true,

(For indeed Nature nor in form nor hue
Bestowed on me her choicest workmanship)
Shall not be thy defence: for, since thy lip
Met mine first, years long past—since thine eye kindled
With soft fire under mine—I have not dwindled,
Nor changed in mind or body, or in aught,
But as love changes what it loveth not
After long years and many trials.
       "How vain
Are words. I thought never to speak again,
Not even in secret, not to my own heart—
But from my lips the unwilling accents start,
And from my pen the words flow as I write,
Dazzling my eyes with scalding tears. My sight
Is dim to see that charactered in vain
On this unfeeling leaf which burns the brain
And eats into it, blotting all things fair
And wise and good which time had written there.
Those who inflict must suffer; for they see
The work of their own hearts, and that must be
Our chastisement or recompense.—O child!
I would that thine were like to be more mild,
For both our wretched sakes—for thine the most,
Who feel'st already all that thou hast lost,
Without the power to wish it thine again.
And, as slow years pass, a funereal train,
Each with the ghost of some lost hope or friend
Following it like its shadow, wilt thou bend
No thought on my dead memory?
       "Alas, love!
Fear me not: against thee I'd not move
A finger in despite. Do I not live
That thou mayst have less bitter cause to grieve?

I give thee tears for scorn, and love for hate ;
And, that thy lot may be less desolate
Than his on whom thus tramplest, I refrain
From that sweet sleep which medicines all pain.
Then—when thou speakest of me—never say
' He could forgive not.'—Here I cast away
All human passions, all revenge, all pride ;
I think, speak, act, no ill ; I do not hide
Under these words, like embers, every spark
Of that which has consumed me. Quick and dark
The grave is yawning : as its roof shall cover
My limbs with dust and worms, under and over,
So let oblivion hide this grief.—The air
Closes upon my accents, as despair
Upon my heart—let death upon despair ! "

He ceased, and overcome leant back awhile ;
Then rising, with a melancholy smile,
Went to a sofa, and lay down, and slept
A heavy sleep ; and in his dreams he wept,
And muttered some familiar name, and we
Wept without shame in his society.
I think I never was impressed so much ;
The man who were not must have lacked a touch
Of human nature.
     Then we lingered not,
Although our argument was quite forgot ;
But, calling the attendants, went to dine
At Maddalo's. Yet neither cheer nor wine
Could give us spirits ; for we talked of him,
And nothing else, till daylight made stars dim.
And we agreed it was some dreadful ill
Wrought on him boldly, yet unspeakable,
By a dear friend ; some deadly change in love

Of one vowed deeply (which he dreamed not of),
For whose sake he, it seemed, had fixed a blot
Of falsehood in his mind, which flourished not
But in the light of all-beholding truth ;
And, having stamped this canker on his youth,
She had abandoned him. And how much more
Might be his woe we guessed not. He had store
Of friends and fortune once, as we could guess
From his nice habits and his gentleness:
These now were lost—it were a grief indeed
If he had changed one unsustaining reed
For all that such a man might else adorn.
The colours of his mind seemed yet unworn ;
For the wild language of his grief was high—
Such as in measure were called poetry.
And I remember one remark which then
Maddalo made: he said—"Most wretched men
Are cradled into poetry by wrong:
They learn in suffering what they teach in song."

If I had been an unconnected man,
I, from this moment, should have formed some plan
Never to leave sweet Venice. For to me
It was delight to ride by the lone sea:
And then the town is silent—one may write
Or read in gondolas, by day or night,
Having the little brazen lamp alight,
Unseen, uninterrupted. Books are there,
Pictures, and casts from all those statues fair
Which were twin-born with poetry, and all
We see in towns, with little to recall
Regret for the green country. I might sit
In Maddalo's great palace, and his wit
And subtle talk would cheer the winter night,

And make me know myself: and the fire-light
Would flash upon our faces, till the day
Might dawn, and make me wonder at my stay.
But I had friends in London too. The chief
Attraction here was that I sought relief
From the deep tenderness that maniac wrought
Within me. . . . 'Twas perhaps an idle thought,
But I imagined that—if day by day
I watchèd him, and seldom went away,
And studied all the beatings of his heart
With zeal (as men study some stubborn art
For their own good), and could by patience find
An entrance to the caverns of his mind—
I might reclaim him from his dark estate.
In friendship I had been most fortunate;
Yet never saw I one whom I would call
More willingly my friend.—And this was all
Accomplished not. Such dreams of baseless good
Oft come and go, in crowds or solitude,
And leave no trace: but what I now designed
Made, for long years, impression on my mind.
The following morning, urged by my affairs,
I left bright Venice.
     After many years
And many changes, I returned. The name
Of Venice, and its aspect, was the same.
But Maddalo was travelling, far away,
Among the mountains of Armenia:
His dog was dead: his child had now become
A woman, such as it has been my doom
To meet with few; a wonder of this earth,
Where there is little of transcendent worth—
Like one of Shakespeare's women. Kindly she,
And with a manner beyond courtesy,

Received her father's friend; and, when I asked
Of the lorn maniac, she her memory tasked,
And told, as she had heard, the mournful tale
That the poor sufferer's health began to fail
Two years from my departure; but that then
The lady who had left him came again.
"Her mien had been imperious, but she now
Looked meek; perhaps remorse had brought her low.
Her coming made him better; and they stayed
Together at my father's—(for I played,
As I remember, with the lady's shawl;
I might be six years old).—But, after all,
She left him."
        "Why, her heart must have been tough!
How did it end?"
        "And was not this enough?
They met, they parted."
        "Child, is there no more?"

"Something within that interval which bore
The stamp of *why* they parted, *how* they met.—
Yet, if thine aged eyes disdain to wet
Those wrinkled cheeks with youth's remembered tears,
Ask me no more; but let the silent years
Be closed and cered over their memory—
As yon mute marble where their corpses lie."

I urged and questioned still. She told me how
All happened—But the cold world shall not know.

POEMS WRITTEN IN 1817.

MARIANNE'S DREAM.

1. A PALE Dream came to a Lady fair,
    And said, "A boon, a boon, I pray!
 I know the secrets of the air;
    And things are lost in the glare of day,
 Which I can make the sleeping see
 If they will put their trust in me.

2. "And thou shalt know of things unknown,
    If thou wilt let me rest between
 The veiny lids whose fringe is thrown
    Over thine eyes so dark and sheen."
 And half in hope and half in fright
 The Lady closed her eyes so bright.

3. At first all deadly shapes were driven
    Tumultuously across her sleep,
 And o'er the vast cope of bending heaven
    All ghastly-visaged clouds did sweep;
 And the Lady ever looked to spy
 If the golden sun shone forth on high.

4. And, as towards the east she turned,
   She saw, aloft in the morning air
 Which now with hues of sunrise burned,
   A great black anchor rising there;
 And wherever the Lady turned her eyes
 It hung before her in the skies.

5. The sky was blue as the summer sea;
   The depths were cloudless overhead;
 The air was calm as it could be;
   There was no sight or sound of dread.
 But that black anchor floating still
 Over the piny eastern hill.

6. The Lady grew sick with a weight of fear
   To see that anchor ever hanging,
 And veiled her eyes. She then did hear
   The sound as of a dim low clanging;
 And looked abroad if she might know
 Was it aught else, or but the flow
 Of the blood in her own veins to and fro.

7. There was a mist in the sunless air,
   Which shook as it were with an earthquake shock;
 But the very weeds that blossomed there
   Were moveless, and each mighty rock
 Stood on its basis steadfastly;
 The anchor was seen no more on high.

8. But piled around, with summits hid
   In lines of cloud at intervals,
 Stood many a mountain pyramid,
   Among whose everlasting walls

Two mighty cities shone, and ever
Through the red mist their domes did quiver.

9. On two dread mountains, from whose crest
    Might seem the eagle for her brood
Would ne'er have hung her dizzy nest,
    Those tower-encircled cities stood.
A vision strange such towers to see,
Sculptured and wrought so gorgeously,
Where human art could never be.

10. And columns framed of marble white,
    And giant fanes, dome over dome
Piled, and triumphant gates, all bright
    With workmanship which could not come
From touch of mortal instrument,
Shot o'er the vales, or lustre lent
From their own shapes magnificent.

11. But still the Lady heard that clang
    Filling the wide air far away,
And still the mist whose light did hang
    Among the mountains shook alway ;
So that the Lady's heart beat fast,
As half in joy and half aghast
On those high domes her look she cast.

12. Sudden from out that city sprung
    A light that made the earth grow red ;
Two flames that each with quivering tongue
    Licked its high domes, and overhead
Among those mighty towers and fanes
Dropped fire, as a volcano rains
It sulphurous ruin on the plains.

13. And hark! a rush, as if the deep
 Had burst its bonds! She looked behind,
And saw over the western steep
 A raging flood descend, and wind
Through that wide vale. She felt no fear,
But said within herself, " 'Tis clear
These towers are Nature's own, and she
To save them has sent forth the sea,"

14. And now those raging billows came
 Where that fair Lady sate; and she
Was borne towards the showering flame
 By the wild waves heaped tumultuously,
And, on a little plank, the flow
Of the whirlpool bore her to and fro.

15. The flames were fiercely vomited
 From every tower and every dome,
And dreary light did wildly shed
 O'er that vast flood's suspended foam
Beneath the smoke which hung its night
On the stained cope of heaven's light.

16. The plank whereon that Lady sate   [about,
 Was driven through the chasms, about and
Between the peaks so desolate
 Of the drowning mountains, in and out,
As the thistle-beard on a whirlwind sails—
While the flood was filling those hollow vales.

17. At last her plank an eddy crossed,
 And bore her to the city's wall,
Which now the flood had reached almost;
 It might the stoutest heart appal

To hear the fire roar and hiss
Through the domes of those mighty palaces.

18. The eddy whirled her round and round
Before a gorgeous gate which stood
Piercing the cloud of smoke which bound
Its aery arch with light like blood.
She looked on that gate of marble clear
With wonder that extinguished fear—

19. For it was filled with sculptures rarest
Of forms most beautiful and strange,
Like nothing human, but the fairest,
Of wingèd shapes whose legions range
Throughout the sleep of those that are,
Like this same Lady, good and fair.

20. And, as she looked, still lovelier grew
Those marble forms; the sculptor sure
Was a strong spirit, and the hue
Of his own mind did there endure
After the touch whose power had braided
Such grace was in some sad change faded.

21. She looked. The flames were dim, the flood
Grew tranquil as a woodland river·
Winding through hills in solitude;
Those marble shapes then seemed to quiver,
And their fair limbs to float in motion
Like weeds unfolding in the ocean.

22. And their lips moved—one seemed to speak—
When suddenly the mountain cracked,

And though the chasm the flood did break
   With an earth-uplifting cataract.
The statues gave a joyous scream—
And on its wings the pale thin Dream
Lifted the Lady from the stream.

23. The dizzy flight of that phantom pale
      Waked the fair Lady from her sleep;
   And she arose, while from the veil
      Of her dark eyes the Dream did creep,
   And she walked about as one who knew
   That sleep has sights as clear and true
   As any waking eyes can view.

Marlow.

DEATH.

THEY die—the dead return not. Misery
      Sits near an open grave, and calls them over,
A youth with hoary hair and haggard eye.
   They are the names of kindred, friend, and lover,
Which he so feebly calls. They all are gone,
Fond wretch, all dead! Those vacant names alone,
   This most familiar scene, my pain,
      These tombs—alone remain.

Misery, my sweetest friend, oh, weep no more!
   Thou wilt not be consoled! I wonder not:
For I have seen thee from thy dwelling's door
   Watch the calm sunset with them, and this spot

Was even as bright and calm but transitory—
And now thy hopes are gone, thy hair is hoary.
  This most familiar scene, my pain,
    These tombs—alone remain.

TO CONSTANTIA, SINGING.

1. THUS to be lost and thus to sink and die
     Perchance were death indeed!—Constantia, turn!
In thy dark eyes a power like light doth lie,
    Even though the sounds which were thy voice, which burn
      Between thy lips, are laid to sleep;
Within thy breath, and on thy hair, like odour, it is yet,
      And from thy touch like fire doth leap.
Even while I write, my burning cheeks are wet;
Alas, that the torn heart can bleed but not forget!

  2. A breathless awe, like the swift change
      Unseen but felt in youthful slumbers,
Wild, sweet, but uncommunicably strange,
Thou breathest now in fast-ascending numbers.
    The cope of heaven seems rent and cloven
      By the enchantment of thy strain,
    And on my shoulders wings are woven,
      To follow its sublime career
        Beyond the mighty moons that wane
Upon the verge of Nature's utmost sphere,
Till the world's shadowy walls are past and disappear.

3. Her voice is hovering o'er my soul—it lingers
    O'ershadowing it with soft and lulling wings :
The blood and life within those snowy fingers
    Teach witchcraft to the instrumental strings.
      My brain is wild, my breath comes quick—
        The blood is listening in my frame,
      And thronging shadows, fast and thick,
        Fall on my overflowing eyes ;
      My heart is quivering like a flame ;
As morning dew that in the sunbeam dies,
I am dissolved in these consuming ecstasies.

4. I have no life, Constantia, now, but thee,
    Whilst, like the world-surrounding air, thy song
Flows on, and fills all things with melody.
    Now is thy voice a tempest swift and strong,
      On which, like one in trance upborne,
      Secure o'er rocks and waves I sweep,
      Rejoicing like a cloud of morn :
      Now 'tis the breath of summer night,
      Which, when the starry waters sleep,
Round western isles with incense-blossoms bright
Lingering, suspends my soul in its voluptuous flight.

SONNET.—OZYMANDIAS.

I MET a traveller from an antique land
    Who said : "Two vast and trunkless legs of stone
Stand in the desert. Near them on the sand,
    Half sunk, a shattered visage lies, whose frown
And wrinkled lip and sneer of cold command

Tell that its sculptor well those passions read
  Which yet survive, stamped on these lifeless things,
The hand that mocked them and the heart that fed.
And on the pedestal these words appear:
  'My name is Ozymandias, king of kings:
Look on my works, ye mighty, and despair!'
  Nothing beside remains. Round the decay
Of that colossal wreck, boundless and bare,
  The lone and level sands stretch far away."

TO THE LORD CHANCELLOR.

1. THY country's curse is on thee, darkest crest
      Of that foul, knotted, many-headed worm
   Which rends our Mother's bosom—priestly pest!
      Masked resurrection of a buried form!

2. Thy country's curse is on thee! Justice sold,
      Truth trampled, Nature's landmarks overthrown,
   And heaps of fraud-accumulated gold,
      Plead, loud as thunder, at Destruction's throne.

3. And, whilst that slow sure Angel which aye stands
      Watching the beck of Mutability
   Delays to execute her high commands,
      And, though a nation weeps, spares thine and thee;

4. Oh, let a father's curse be on thy soul,
      And let a daughter's hope be on thy tomb,
   And both on thy grey head a leaden cowl
      To weigh thee down to thine approaching doom!

5. I curse thee by a parent's outraged love ;
    By hopes long cherished and too lately lost ;
  By gentle feelings thou couldst never prove ;
    By griefs which thy stern nature never crossed ;

6. By those infantine smiles of happy light
    Which were a fire within a stranger's hearth,
  Quenched even when kindled, in untimely night
    Hiding the promise of a lovely birth ;

7. By those unpractised accents of young speech,
    Which he who is a father thought to frame
  To gentlest lore such as the wisest teach.   [shame !
    Thou strike the lyre of mind ! Oh grief and

8. By all the happy see in children's growth,
    That undeveloped flower of budding years,
  Sweetness and sadness interwoven both,
    Source of the sweetest hopes and saddest fears :

9. By all the days, under a hireling's care,
    Of dull constraint and bitter heaviness—
  Oh wretched ye if ever any were,
    Sadder than orphans yet not fatherless—

10. By the false cant which on their innocent lips
    Must hang like poison on an opening bloom ;
  By the dark creeds which cover with eclipse
    Their pathway from the cradle to the tomb ;

11. By thy most impious hell, and all its terrors ;
    By all the grief, the madness, and the guilt
  Of thine impostures, which must be their errors,
    That sand on which thy crumbling power is built ;

12. By thy complicity with lust and hate,
      Thy thirst for tears, thy hunger after gold,
   The ready frauds which ever on thee wait,
      The servile arts in which thou hast grown old ;

13. By thy most killing sneer, and by thy smile,
      By all the acts and snares of thy black den,
   And—for thou canst outweep the crocodile—
      By thy false tears, those millstones braining men ;

14. By all the hate which checks a father's love ;
      By all the scorn which kills a father's care ;
   By those most impious hands that dared remove
      Nature's high bounds ; by thee ; and by despair—

15. Yes, the despair which bids a father groan,
      And cry, "My children are no longer mine ;
   The blood within those veins may be mine own,
      But, tyrant, their polluted souls are thine !"

16. I curse thee, though I hate thee not. O slave !
      If thou couldst quench the earth-consuming hell
   Of which thou art a demon, on thy grave
      This curse should be a blessing. Fare thee well !

TO WILLIAM SHELLEY.

1. THE billows on the beach are leaping around it ;
      The bark is weak and frail ;
   The sea looks black, and the clouds that bound it
      Darkly strew the gale.

Come with me, thou delightful child,
Come with me! Though the wave is wild,
And the winds are loose, we must not stay,
Or the slaves of law may rend thee away.

2. They have taken thy brother and sister dear,
   They have made them unfit for thee;
They have withered the smile and dried the tear
   Which should have been sacred to me.
To a blighting faith and a cause of crime
They have bound them slaves in youthly time;
And they will curse my name and thee
Because we fearless are and free.

3. Come thou, beloved as thou art!
   Another sleepeth still
Near thy sweet mother's anxious heart,
   Which thou with joy wilt fill,
With fairest smiles of wonder thrown
On that which is indeed our own,
And which in distant lands will be
The dearest playmate unto thee.

4. Fear not the tyrants will rule for ever,
   Or the priests of the evil faith;
They stand on the brink of that raging river
   Whose waves they have tainted with death.
It is fed from the depth of a thousand dells,
Around them it foams, and rages, and swells;
And their swords and their sceptres I floating see,
Like wrecks, on the surge of eternity.

5. Rest, rest, shriek not, thou gentle child!
   The rocking of the boat thou fearest,

And the cold spray and the clamour wild!
  There! sit between us two, thou dearest—
Me and thy mother. Well we know
The storm at which thou tremblest so,
With all its dark and hungry graves,
Less cruel than the savage slaves
Who hunt thee o'er these sheltering waves.

6. This hour will in thy memory
    Be a dream of days forgotten;
We soon shall dwell by the azure sea
Of serene and golden Italy,
Or Greece the mother of the free.
And I will teach thine infant tongue
To call upon their heroes old
In their own language, and will mould
Thy growing spirit in the flame
Of Grecian lore; that by such name
A patriot's birthright thou mayst claim.

LINES.

THAT time is dead for ever, child,
  Drowned, frozen, dead for ever!
    We look on the past;
    And stare aghast
At the spectres, wailing, pale, and ghast,
Of hopes which thou and I beguiled
    To death on life's dark river.

The stream we gazed on then rolled by ;
　Its waves are unreturning ;
　　But we yet stand
　　In a lone land,
Like tombs to mark the memory
Of hopes and fears which fade and fly
　In the light of life's dim morning.

5th November 1817.

ON FANNY GODWIN.

HER voice did quiver as we parted ;
　　Yet knew I not that heart was broken
From which it came, and I departed
　Heeding not the words then spoken.
Misery—O Misery,
This world is all too wide for thee !

LINES TO A CRITIC.

1. HONEY from silkworms who can gather
　　Or silk from the yellow bee ?
　The grass may grow in winter weather
　　As soon as hate in me.

2. Hate men who cant, and men who pray,
　　And men who rail, like thee ;
　An equal passion to repay
　　They are not coy like me.

LINES TO A CRITIC.

3. Or seek some slave of power and gold
   To be thy dear heart's mate;
   Thy love will move that bigot cold
   Sooner than me thy hate.

4. A passion like the one I prove
   Cannot divided be;
   I hate thy want of truth and love—
   How should I then hate thee?

December 1817.

POEMS WRITTEN IN 1818.

PASSAGE OF THE APENNINES.

LISTEN, listen, Mary mine,
   To the whisper of the Apennine.
It bursts on the roof like the thunder's roar;
Or like the sea on a northern shore,
Heard in its raging ebb and flow
By the captives pent in the cave below.
The Apennine in the light of day
Is a mighty mountain dim and grey
Which between the earth and sky doth lay:
But, when night comes, a chaos dread
On the dim starlight then is spread,
And the Apennine walks abroad with the storm.

4th May 1818.

ON A DEAD VIOLET.

To Miss ——.

THE odour from the flower is gone
    Which like thy kisses breathed on me;
The colour from the flower is flown
    Which glowed of thee and only thee!

A shrivelled, lifeless, vacant form,
    It lies on my abandoned breast;
And mocks the heart, which yet is warm
    With cold and silent rest.

I weep—my tears revive it not;
    I sigh—it breathes no more on me:
Its mute and uncomplaining lot
    Is such as mine should be.

THE PAST.

WILT thou forget the happy hours
    Which we buried in Love's sweet bowers,
Heaping over their corpses cold
Blossoms and leaves instead of mould?
Blossoms which were the joys that fell,
    And leaves, the hopes that yet remain.

Forget the dead, the past? Oh yet
There are ghosts that may take revenge for it!

Memories that make the heart a tomb,
Regrets which glide through the spirit's gloom,
And with ghastly whispers tell
    That joy, once lost, is pain.

SONNET.

LIFT not the painted veil which those who live
    Call Life; though unreal shapes be pictured there,
And it but mimic all we would believe
    With colours idly spread. Behind, lurk Fear
And Hope, twin Destinies, who ever weave
    Their shadows o'er the chasm sightless and drear.
I knew one who had lifted it—he sought,
    For his lost heart was tender, things to love,
But found them not, alas! nor was there aught
    The world contains in which he could approve.
Through the unheeding many he did move,
A splendour among shadows, a bright blot
    Upon this gloomy scene, a spirit that strove
For truth, and, like the Preacher, found it not.

LINES WRITTEN AMONG THE EUGANEAN HILLS.

MANY a green isle needs must be
    In the deep wide sea of Misery;
Or the mariner, worn and wan,
Never thus could voyage on—

THE EUGANEAN HILLS.

Day and night, and night and day.
Drifting on his dreary way,
With the solid darkness black
Closing round his vessel's track ;
Whilst, above, the sunless sky,
Big with clouds, hangs heavily—
And, behind, the tempest fleet
Hurries on with lightning feet,
Riving sail and cord and plank,
Till the ship has almost drank
Death from the o'er-brimming deep,
And sinks down, down, like that sleep
When the dreamer seems to be
Weltering through eternity,
And the dim low line before
Of a dark and distant shore
Still recedes, as—ever still
Longing with divided will,
But no power to seek or shun—
He is ever drifted on
O'er the unreposing wave
To the haven of the grave.
What if there no friends will greet ?
What if there no heart will meet
His with love's impatient beat ?
Wander wheresoe'er he may,
Can he dream before that day
To find refuge from distress
In friendship's smile, in love's caress ?
Then 'twill wreak him little woe
Whether such there be or no.
Senseless is the breast, and cold,
Which relenting love would fold ;
Bloodless are the veins, and chill,

Which the pulse of pain did fill;
Every little living nerve
That from bitter words did swerve
Round the tortured lips and brow
Is like a sapless leaflet now
Frozen upon December's bough.

On the beach of a northern sea
Which tempests shake eternally
As once the wretch there lay to sleep,
Lies a solitary heap,
One white skull and seven dry bones,
On the margin of the stones,
Where a few grey rushes stand,
Boundaries of the sea and land.
Nor is heard one voice of wail
But the sea-mews' as they sail
O'er the billows of the gale,
Or the whirlwind up and down
Howling—like a slaughtered town,
Where a king in glory rides
Through the pomp of fratricides.
Those unburied bones around
There is many a mournful sound;
There is no lament for him,
Like a sunless vapour, dim,
Who once clothed with life and thought
What now moves nor murmurs not.

Ay, many flowering islands lie
In the waters of wide Agony—
To such a one this morn was led
My bark, by soft winds piloted.
'Mid the mountains Euganean,

THE EUGANEAN HILLS.

I stood listening to the pæan
With which the legioned rooks did hail
The sun's uprise majestical.
Gathering round with wings all hoar,
Through the dewy mist they soar
Like grey shades, till the eastern heaven
Bursts; and then, as clouds of even
Flecked with fire and azure lie
In the unfathomable sky,
So their plumes of purple grain,
Starred with drops of golden rain,
Gleam above the sunlight woods,
As in silent multitudes
On the morning's fitful gale
Through the broken mist they sail,
And the vapours cloven and gleaming
Follow, down the dark steep streaming—
Till all is bright, and clear, and still
Round the solitary hill.

Beneath is spread like a green sea
The waveless plain of Lombardy,
Bounded by the vaporous air,
Islanded by cities fair.
Underneath Day's azure eyes,
Ocean's nursling, Venice lies—
A peopled labyrinth of walls,
Amphitrite's destined halls,
Which her hoary sire now paves
With his blue and beaming waves.
Lo! the sun upsprings behind,
Broad, red, radiant, half-reclined
On the level quivering line
Of the waters crystalline;

And before that chasm of light,
As within a furnace bright,
Column, tower, and dome, and spire,
Shine like obelisks of fire,
Pointing with inconstant motion
From the altar of dark ocean
To the sapphire-tinted skies;
As the flames of sacrifice
From the marble shrines did rise,
As to pierce the dome of gold
Where Apollo spoke of old.

Sun-girt City! thou hast been
Ocean's child, and then his queen.
Now is come a darker day;
And thou soon must be his prey,
If the power that raised thee here
Hallow so thy watery bier.
A less drear ruin then than now,
With thy conquest-branded brow
Stooping to the slave of slaves
From thy throne, among the waves
Wilt thou be when the sea-mew
Flies, as once before it flew,
O'er thine isles depopulate,
And all is in its ancient state;
Save where many a palace-gate
With green sea-flowers overgrown
Like a rock of ocean's own,
Topples o'er the abandoned sea
As the tides change sullenly.
The fisher on his watery way
Wandering at the close of day
Will spread his sail and seize his oar

THE EUGANEAN HILLS.

Till he pass the gloomy shore,
Lest thy dead should, from their sleep
Bursting o'er the starlight deep,
Lead a rapid masque of death
O'er the waters of his path.

Those who alone thy towers behold
Quivering through aërial gold,
As I now behold them here,
Would imagine not they were
Sepulchres where human forms,
Like pollution-nourished worms,
To the corpse of greatness cling,
Murdered and now mouldering.
But, if Freedom should awake
In her omnipotence, and shake
From the Celtic Anarch's hold
All the keys of dungeons cold
Where a hundred cities lie
Chained like thee ingloriously,
Thou and all thy sister band
Might adorn this sunny land,
Twining memories of old time
With new virtues more sublime.
If not, perish thou and they—
Clouds which stain truth's rising day,
By her sun consumed away!
E'en can spare ye; while like flowers,
In the waste of years and hours,
From your dust new nations spring
With more kindly blossoming.

Perish! Let there only be,
Floating o'er thy hearthless sea

As the garment of thy sky
Clothes the world immortally,
One remembrance, more sublime
Than the tattered pall of time
Which scarce hides thy visage wan:
That a tempest-cleaving swan
Of the songs of Albion,
Driven from his ancestral streams
By the might of evil dreams,
Found a nest in thee; and ocean
Welcomed him with such emotion
That its joy grew his, and sprung
From his lips like music flung
O'er a mighty thunder-fit,
Chastening terror.   What though yet
Poesy's unfailing river,
Which through Albion winds for ever,
Lashing with melodious wave
Many a sacred poet's grave,
Mourn its latest nursling fled!
What though thou with all thy dead
Scarce canst for this fame repay
Aught thine own—oh! rather say,
Though thy sins and slaveries foul
Overcloud a sunlike soul?
As the ghost of Homer clings
Round Scamander's wasting springs;
As divinest Shakespeare's might
Fills Avon and the world with light,
Like Omniscient Power, which he
Imaged 'mid mortality;
As the love from Petrarch's urn
Yet amid yon hills doth burn,
A quenchless lamp by which the heart

Sees things unearthly; so thou art,
Mighty spirit! so shall be
The city that did refuge thee!

Lo, the sun floats up the sky,
Like thought-wingèd Liberty,
Till the universal light
Seems to level plain and height.
From the sea a mist has spread,
And the beams of morn lie dead
On the towers of Venice now,
Like its glory long ago.
By the skirts of that grey cloud
Many-domèd Padua proud
Stands, a peopled solitude
'Mid the harvest-shining plain;
Where the peasant heaps his grain
In the garner of his foe,
And the milk-white oxen slow
With the purple vintage strain
Heaped upon the creaking wain,
That the brutal Celt may swill
Drunken sleep with savage will.
And the sickle to the sword
Lies unchanged, though many a lord,
Like a weed whose shade is poison,
Overgrows this region's foison,
Sheaves of whom are ripe to come
To destruction's harvest-home.
Men must reap the things they sow
Force from force must ever flow,
Or worse: but 'tis a bitter woe
That love or reason cannot change
The despot's rage, the slave's revenge.

Padua! (thou within whose walls
Those mute guests at festivals,
Son and Mother, Death and Sin,
Played at dice for Ezzelin,
Till Death cried, "I win, I win!"
And Sin cursed to lose the wager;
But Death promised, to assuage her,
That he would petition for
Her to be made Vice-Emperor,
When the destined years were o'er,
Over all between the Po
And the eastern Alpine snow,
Under the mighty Austrian:
Sin smiled so as Sin only can;
And, since that time, ay long before
Both have ruled from shore to shore,
That incestuous pair who follow
Tyrants as the sun the swallow,
As repentance follows crime,
And as changes follow time)—
In thine halls the lamp of learning,
Padua, now no more is burning.
Like a meteor whose wild way
Is lost over the grave of day,
It gleams betrayed and to betray.
Once remotest nations came
To adore that sacred flame,
When it lit not many a hearth
On this cold and gloomy earth;
Now new fires from antique light
Spring beneath the wide world's might—
But their spark lies dead in thee,
Trampled out by Tyranny.

As the Norway woodman quells,
In the depth of piny dells,
One light flame among the brakes,
While the boundless forest shakes,
And its mighty trunks are torn
By the fire thus lowly born—
The spark beneath his feet is dead;
He starts to see the flames it fed
Howling through the darkened sky
With myriad tongues victoriously,
And sinks down in fear—so thou,
O Tyranny! beholdest now
Light around thee, and thou hearest
The loud flames ascend, and fearest.
Grovel on the earth! ay, hide
In the dust thy purple pride!

Noon descends around me now.
'Tis the noon of autumn's glow;
When a soft and purple mist,
Like a vaporous amethyst,
Or an air-dissolvèd star
Mingling light and fragrance, far
From the curved horizon's bound
To the point of heaven's profound
Fills the overflowing sky.
And the plains that silent lie
Underneath; the leaves unsodden
Where the infant Frost has trodden
With his morning-wingèd feet
Whose bright print is gleaming yet;
And the red and golden vines,
Piercing with their trellised lines
The rough dark-skirted wilderness;

The dun and bladed grass no less,
Pointing from this hoary tower
In the windless air; the flower
Glimmering at my feet; the line
Of the olive-sandalled Apennine
In the south dimly islanded;
And the Alps, whose snows are spread
High between the clouds and sun;
And of living things each one;
And my spirit, which so long
Darkened this swift stream of song—
Interpenetrated lie
By the glory of the sky:
Be it love, light, harmony,
Odour, or the soul of all
Which from heaven like dew doth fall,
Or the mind which feeds this verse
Peopling the lone universe.

Noon descends; and after noon
Autumn's evening meets me soon,
Leading the infantine moon,
And that one star which to her
Almost seems to minister
Half the crimson light she brings
From the sunset's radiant springs.
And the soft dreams of the morn
(Which like winged winds had borne,
To that silent isle which lies
'Mid remembered agonies,
The frail bark of this lone being)
Pass, to other sufferers fleeing;
And its ancient pilot, Pain,
Sits beside the helm again.

THE EUGANEAN HILLS.

Other flowering isles must be
In the sea of Life and Agony:
Other spirits float and flee
O'er that gulf. Even now perhaps
On some rock the wild wave wraps,
With folded wings, they waiting sit
For my bark, to pilot it
To some calm and blooming cove;
Where for me and those I love
May a windless bower be built,
Far from passion, pain, and guilt,
In a dell 'mid lawny hills
Which the wild sea-murmur fills,
And soft sunshine, and the sound
Of old forests echoing round,
And the light and smell divine
Of all flowers that breathe and shine.
We may live so happy there
That the Spirits of the Air,
Envying us, may even entice
To our healing paradise
The polluting multitude.
But their rage would be subdued
By that clime divine and calm,
And the winds whose wings rain balm
On the uplifted soul, and leaves
Under which the bright sea heaves;
While each breathless interval
In their whisperings musical
The inspirèd soul supplies
With its own deep melodies,
And the love which heals all strife,
Circling, like the breath of life,
All things in that sweet abode

With its own mild brotherhood.
They, not it, would change; and soon
Every sprite beneath the moon
Would repent its envy vain,
And the earth grow young again.

October 1818.

STANZAS

WRITTEN IN DEJECTION NEAR NAPLES.

1. THE sun is warm, the sky is clear
      The waves are dancing fast and bright;
    Blue isles and snowy mountains wear
      The purple noon's transparent might;
      The breath of the moist earth is light
    Around its unexpanded buds;
      Like many a voice of one delight,
    The winds', the birds', the ocean floods',
    The city's voice itself, is soft like Solitude's.

2. I see the deep's untrampled floor
      With green and purple sea-weed strown;
    I see the waves upon the shore,
      Like light dissolved, in star-showers thrown.
      I sit upon the sands alone.
    The lightning of the noontide ocean
      Is flashing round me, and a tone
    Arises from its measured motion—
    How sweet, did any heart now share in my emotion!

3. Alas! I have nor hope nor health,
   Nor peace within nor calm around;
Nor that content, surpassing wealth,
   The sage in meditation found,
   And walked with inward glory crowned;
Nor fame, nor power, nor love, nor leisure.
   Others I see whom these surround—
Smiling they live, and call life pleasure;
To me that cup has been dealt in another measure.

4. Yet now despair itself is mild,
   Even as the winds and waters are;
I could lie down like a tired child,
   And weep away the life of care
   Which I have borne and yet must bear—
Till death like sleep might steal on me,
   And I might feel in the warm air
My cheek grow cold, and hear the sea
Breathe o'er my dying brain its last monotony.

5. Some might lament that I were cold,
   As I when this sweet day is gone,
Which my lost heart, too soon grown old,
   Insults with this untimely moan.
   They might lament—for I am one
Whom men love not, and yet regret;
   Unlike this day, which, when the sun
Shall on its stainless glory set,
Will linger, though enjoyed, like joy in memory yet.

December 1818.

MISERY.

1. COME, be happy—sit near me,
    Shadow-vested Misery:
   Coy, unwilling, silent bride,
   Mourning in thy robe of pride,
   Desolation deified !

2. Come, be happy—sit near me :
   Sad as I may seem to thee,
   I am happier far than thou,
   Lady whose imperial brow
   Is endiademed with woe.

3. Misery ! we have known each other,
   Like a sister and a brother
   Living in the same lone home,
   Many years : we must live some
   Hours or ages yet to come.

4. 'Tis an evil lot, and yet
   Let us make the best of it ;
   If love can live when pleasure dies,
   We two will love, till in our eyes
   This heart's hell seem paradise.

5. Come, be happy—lie thee down
   On the fresh grass newly mown,
   Where the grasshopper doth sing
   Merrily—one joyous thing
   In a world of sorrowing.

6. There our tent shall be the willow,
   And mine arm shall be thy pillow:
   Sounds and odours, sorrowful
   Because they once were sweet, shall lull
   Us to slumber deep and dull.

7. Ha! thy frozen pulses flutter
   With a love thou dar'st not utter.
   Thou art murmuring—thou art weeping—
   Is thine icy bosom leaping,
   While my burning heart lies sleeping?

8. Kiss me—oh! thy lips are cold!
   Round my neck thine arms enfold—
   They are soft, but chill and dead;
   And thy tears upon my head
   Burn like points of frozen lead.

9. Hasten to the bridal bed—
   Underneath the grave 'tis spread:
   In darkness may our love be hid,
   Oblivion be our coverlid—
   May we rest, and none forbid.

10. Clasp me, till our hearts be grown
    Like two lovers into one;
    Till this dreadful transport may
    Like a vapour fade away
    In the sleep that lasts alway.

11. We may dream in that long sleep
    That we are not those who weep;

Even as Pleasure dreams of thee,
Life-deserting Misery,
Thou mayst dream of her with me.

12. Let us laugh and make our mirth
At the shadows of the earth;
As dogs bay the moonlight clouds
Which, like spectres wrapped in shrouds,
Pass o'er night in multitudes.

13. All the wide world, beside us,
Show like multitudinous
Puppets passing from a scene;
But what mockery can they mean
Where I am—where thou hast been?

THE WITCH OF ATLAS.

TO MARY.

(On her objecting to the following poem, upon the score of its containing no human interest.)

1. HOW, my dear Mary, are you critic-bitten
    (For vipers kill, though dead) by some review—
  That you condemn these verses I have written,
    Because they tell no story, false or true?
  What though no mice are caught by a young kitten?
    May it not leap and play as grown cats do,
  Till its claws come? Prithee, for this one time,
  Content thee with a visionary rhyme.

2. What hand would crush the silken-wingèd fly,
    The youngest of inconstant April's minions,
  Because it cannot climb the purest sky,
    Where the swan sings amid the sun's dominions?
  Not thine. Thou knowest 'tis its doom to die
    When Day shall hide within her twilight pinions
  The lucent eyes and the eternal smile,
  Serene as thine, which lent it life while.

3. To thy fair feet a wingèd Vision came,
    Whose date should have been longer than a day,

And o'er thy head did beat its wings for fame,
　　And in thy sight its fading plumes display;
The watery bow burned in the evening flame;
　　But the shower fell, the swift Sun went his way—
And that is dead.　Oh let me not believe
That anything of mine is fit to live !

4.　Wordsworth informs us he was nineteen years
　　　Considering and retouching Peter Bell ;
Watering his laurels with the killing tears
　　Of slow dull care, so that their roots to hell
Might pierce, and their wide branches blot the spheres
　　Of heaven with dewy leaves and flowers : this well
May be, for heaven and earth conspire to foil
The over-busy gardener's blundering toil.

5.　My Witch indeed is not so sweet a creature
　　　As Ruth or Lucy, whom his graceful praise
Clothes for our grandsons—but she matches Peter,
　　Though he took nineteen years, and she three days,
In dressing.　Light the vest of flowing metre
　　She wears: he, proud as dandy with his stays,
Has hung upon his wiry limbs a dress
Like King Lear's looped and windowed raggedness.

6.　If you strip Peter, you will see a fellow
　　　Scorched by hell's hyperequatorial climate
Into a kind of a sulphureous yellow;
　　A lean mark, hardly fit to fling a rhyme at ;
In shape a Scaramouch, in hue Othello.
　　If you unveil my Witch, no priest nor primate
Can shrive you of that sin—if sin there be
In love when it becomes idolatry.

THE WITCH OF ATLAS.

1. BEFORE those cruel twins whom at one birth
      Incestuous Change bore to her father Time,
   Error and Truth, had hunted from the earth
      All those bright natures which adorned its prime,
   And left us nothing to believe in, worth
      The pains of putting into learned rhyme,
   A Lady Witch there lived on Atlas mountain
   Within a cavern by a secret fountain.

2. Her mother was one of the Atlantides.
      The all-beholding Sun had ne'er beholden
   In his wide voyage o'er continents and seas
      So fair a creature, as she lay enfolden
   In the warm shadow of her loveliness;
      He kissed her with his beams, and made all golden
   The chamber of grey rock in which she lay.
   She, in that dream of joy, dissolved away.

3. 'Tis said she was first changed into a vapour;
      And then into a cloud—such clouds as flit
   (Like splendour-wingèd moths about a taper)
      Round the red west when the Sun dies in it;
   And then into a meteor, such as caper
      On hill-tops when the Moon is in a fit;
   Then into one of those mysterious stars   [Mars.
   Which hide themselves between the Earth and

4. Ten times the Mother of the Months had bent
      Her bow beside the folding-star, and bidden
   With that bright sign the billows to indent
      The sea-deserted sand—(like children chidden,

At her command they ever came and went)—
Since in that cave a dewy splendour hidden
Took shape and motion. With the living form
Of this embodied Power the cave grew warm.

5. A lovely Lady garmented in light
From her own beauty : deep her eyes as are
Two openings of unfathomable night
Seen through a tempest's cloven roof ; her hair
Dark ; the dim brain whirls dizzy with delight,
Picturing her form. Her soft smiles shone afar ;
And her low voice was heard like love, and drew
All living things towards this wonder new.

6. And first the spotted camelopard came ;
And then the wise and fearless elephant ;
Then the sly serpent, in the golden flame
Of his own volumes intervolved. All gaunt
And sanguine beasts her gentle looks made tame—
They drank before her at her sacred fount ;
And every beast of beating heart grew bold,
Such gentleness and power even to behold.

7. The brinded lioness led forth her young,
That she might teach them how they should forego
Their inborn thirst of death ; the pard unstrung
His sinews at her feet, and sought to know,
With looks whose motions spoke without a tongue,
How he might be as gentle as the doe.
The magic circle of her voice and eyes
All savage natures did imparadise.

8. And old Silenus, shaking a green stick
Of lilies, and the Wood-gods in a crew,

Came blithe as in the olive copses thick
    Cicadæ are, drunk with the noonday dew ;
And Dryope and Faunus followed quick,
    Teasing the god to sing them something new ;
Till in this cave they found the Lady lone,
Sitting upon a seat of emerald stone.

9. And universal Pan, 'tis said, was there,
    And, though none saw him—through the adamant
Of the deep mountains, through the trackless air,
    And through those living spirits, like a want—
He passed out of his everlasting lair   [pant,
    Where the quick heart of the great world doth
And felt that wondrous Lady all alone—
And she felt him upon her emerald throne.

10. And every Nymph of stream and spreading tree,
    And every Shepherdess of Ocean's flocks
Who drives her white waves over the green sea,
    And Ocean with the brine on his grey locks,
And quaint Priapus with his company—   [rocks
    All came, much wondering how the enwombèd
Could have brought forth so beautiful a birth :
Her love subdued their wonder and their mirth.

11. The herdsmen and the mountain maidens came,
    And the rude kings of pastoral Garamant—
Their spirits shook within them, as a flame
    Stirred by the air under a cavern gaunt :
Pygmies and Polyphemes, by many a name,
    Centaurs and Satyrs, and such shapes as haunt
Wet clefts—and lumps neither alive nor dead
Dog-headed, bosom-eyed, and bird-footed.

12. For she was beautiful.   Her beauty made
    The bright world dim, and everything beside
Seemed like the fleeting image of a shade.
    No thought of living spirit could abide
(Which to her looks had ever been betrayed)
    On any object in the world so wide,
On any hope within the circling skies—
But on her form, and in her inmost eyes.

13. Which when the Lady knew, she took her spindle,
    And twined three threads of fleecy mist and three
Long lines of light, such as the dawn may kindle
    The clouds, and waves, and mountains with, and she
As many starbeams, ere their lamps could dwindle
    In the belated moon, wound skilfully ;
And with these threads a subtle veil she wove—
A shadow for the splendour of her love.

14. The deep recesses of her odorous dwelling
    Were stored with magic treasures—sounds of air
Which had the power all spirits of compelling,
    Folded in cells of crystal silence there ;
Such as we hear in youth, and think the feeling
    Will never die—yet, ere we are aware,
The feeling and the sound are fled and gone,
And the regret they leave remains alone.

15. And there lay Visions swift, and sweet, and quaint,
    Each in its thin sheath like a chrysalis ;
Some eager to burst forth ; some weak and faint
    With the soft burthen of intensest bliss
It is their work to bear to many a saint
    Whose heart adores the shrine which holiest is,

Even Love's; and others, white, green, grey, and
    black,
And of all shapes—and each was at her beck.

16. And odours in a kind of aviary
        Of ever-blooming Eden-trees she kept,
    Clipped in a floating net a love-sick Fairy
        Had woven from dew-beams while the moon yet
            slept.
    As bats at the wired window of a dairy,
        They beat their vans; and each was an adept—
    When loosed and missioned, making wings of
            winds—
    To stir sweet thoughts or sad in destined minds.

17. And liquors clear and sweet, whose healthful might
        Could medicine the sick soul to happy sleep,
    And change eternal death into a night
        Of glorious dreams—or, if eyes needs must weep,
    Could make their tears all wonder and delight—
        She in her crystal phials did closely keep:
    If men could drink of those clear phials, 'tis said
    The living were not envied of the dead.

18. Her cave was stored with scrolls of strange device,
        The works of some Saturnian Archimage,
    Which taught the expiations at whose price
        Men from the gods might win that happy age
    Too lightly lost, redeeming native vice—
        And which might quench the earth-consuming
            rage
    Of gold and blood, till men should live and move
    Harmonious as the sacred stars above—

19. And how all things that seem untameable,
    Not to be checked and not to be confined,
Obey the spells of Wisdom's wizard skill;
    Time, earth, and fire, the ocean, and the wind,
And all their shapes, and man's imperial will—
    And other scrolls whose writings did unbind
The inmost lore of love—let the profane
Tremble to ask what secrets they contain.

20. And wondrous works of substances unknown,
    To which the enchantment of her Father's power
Had changed those rugged blocks of savage stone,
    Were heaped in the recesses of her bower;
Carved lamps and chalices, and phials which shone
    In their own golden beams—each like a flower
Out of whose depth a fire-fly shakes his light
Under a cypress in a starless night.

21. At first she lived alone in this wild home,
    And her own thoughts were each a minister,
Clothing themselves or with the ocean foam,
    Or with the wind, or with the speed of fire,
To work whatever purposes might come
    Into her mind: such power her mighty Sire
Had girt them with, whether to fly or run
Through all the regions which he shines upon.

22. The Ocean-nymphs and Hamadryades,
    Oreads and Naiads with long weedy locks,
Offered to do her bidding through the seas,
    Under the earth, and in the hollow rocks,
And far beneath the matted roots of trees,
    And in the gnarlèd heart of stubborn oaks;

THE WITCH OF ATLAS.

  So they might live for ever in the light
  Of her sweet presence—each a satellite.

23. "This may not be," the Wizard Maid replied.
  "The fountains where the Naiades bedew
 Their shining hair at length are drained and dried;
  The solid oaks forget their strength, and strew
 Their latest leaf upon the mountains wide;
  The boundless ocean like a drop of dew
 Will be consumed; the stubborn centre must
 Be scattered like a cloud of summer dust.

24. "And ye, with them, will perish one by one.
  If I must sigh to think that this shall be,
 If I must weep when the surviving Sun
  Shall smile on your decay—oh, ask not me
 To love you till your little race is run;
  I cannot die as ye must—Over me [dwell
 Your leaves shall glance—the streams in which ye
 Shall be my paths henceforth; and so farewell!"

25. She spoke and wept. The dark and azure well
  Sparkled beneath the shower of her bright tears,
 And every little circlet where they fell
  Flung to the cavern roof inconstant spheres
 And intertangled lines of light. A knell
  Of sobbing voices came upon her ears
 From those departing forms, o'er the serene
 Of the white streams and of the forest green.

26. All day the Wizard Lady sat aloof;
  Spelling out scrolls of dread antiquity
 Under the cavern's fountain-lighted roof;
  Or broidering the pictured poesy

Of some high tale upon her growing woof,   [dye
  Which the sweet splendour of her smiles could
In hues outshining heaven—and ever she
Added some grace to the wrought poesy—

27. While on her hearth lay blazing many a piece
    Of sandal wood, rare gums, and cinnamon.
  Men scarcely know how beautiful fire is;
    Each flame of it is as a precious stone
Dissolved in ever-moving light, and *this*
    Belongs to each and all who gaze thereon.
The Witch beheld it not, for in her hand
She held a woof that dimmed the burning brand.

28. This Lady never slept, but lay in trance
    All night within the fountain—as in sleep.
  Its emerald crags glowed in her beauty's glance:
    Through the green splendour of the water deep
She saw the constellations reel and dance
    Like fire-flies—and withal did ever keep
The tenor of her contemplations calm,
With open eyes, closed feet, and folded palm.

29. And, when the whirlwinds and the clouds descended
    From the white pinnacles of that cold hill,
  She passed at dewfall to a space extended,
    Where in a lawn of flowering asphodel
Amid a wood of pines and cedars blended,
    There yawned an inextinguishable well
Of crimson fire, full even to the brim,
And overflowing all the margin trim—

30. Within the which she lay when the fierce war
    Of wintry winds shook that innocuous liquor,

THE WITCH OF ATLAS.

In many a mimic moon and bearded star, [flicker
O'er woods and lawns. The serpent heard it
In sleep, and, dreaming still, he crept afar.
And, when the windless snow descended thicker
Than autumn leaves, she watched it as it came
Melt on the surface of the level flame.

31. She had a boat which some say Vulcan wrought
For Venus, as the chariot of her star;
But it was found too feeble to be fraught
With all the ardours in that sphere which are,
And so she sold it, and Apollo bought
And gave it to this daughter: from a car,
Changed to the fairest and the lightest boat
Which ever upon mortal stream did float.

32. And others say that, when but three hours old,
The firstborn Love out of his cradle leapt,
And clove dun chaos with his wings of gold,
And, like a horticultural adept,
Stole a strange seed, and wrapped it up in mould,
And sowed it in his mother's star, and kept
Watering it all the summer with sweet dew,
And with his wings fanning it as it grew.

33. The plant grew strong and green—the snowy flower
Fell, and the long and gourd-like fruit began
To turn the light and dew by inward power
To its own substance: woven tracery ran
Of light firm texture, ribbed and branching, o'er
The solid rind, like a leaf's veinèd fan—
Of which Love scooped this boat, and with soft motion
Piloted it round the circumfluous ocean.

34. This boat she moored upon her fount, and lit
    A living spirit within all its frame,
Breathing the soul of swiftness into it.
    Couched on the fountain—like a panther tame
(One of the twain at Evan's feet that sit),
    Or as on Vesta's sceptre a swift flame,
Or on blind Homer's heart a wingèd thought—
In joyous expectation lay the boat.

35. Then by strange art she kneaded fire and snow
    Together, tempering the repugnant mass
With liquid love—all things together grow
    Through which the harmony of love can pass;
And a fair Shape out of her hands did flow—
    A living image which did far surpass
In beauty that bright shape of vital stone
Which drew the heart out of Pygmalion.

36. A sexless thing it was, and in its growth
    It seemed to have developed no defect
Of either sex, yet all the grace of both.
    In gentleness and strength its limbs were decked;
The bosom lightly swelled with its full youth;
    The countenance was such as might select
Some artist that his skill should never die,
Imaging forth such perfect purity.

37. From its smooth shoulders hung two rapid wings
    Fit to have borne it to the seventh sphere,
Tipped with the speed of liquid lightnings,
    Dyed in the ardours of the atmosphere.
She led her creature to the boiling springs
    Where the light boat was moored, and said "Sit here,"

And pointed to the prow, and took her seat
Beside the rudder with opposing feet.

38. And down the streams which clove those mountains
      vast,
   Around their inland islets, and amid
The panther-peopled forests (whose shade cast
   Darkness and odours, and a pleasure hid
In melancholy gloom) the pinnace passed;
   By many a star-surrounded pyramid
Of icy crag cleaving the purple sky,
And caverns yawning round unfathomably.

39. The silver noon into that winding dell,
   With slanted gleam athwart the forest tops,
Tempered like golden evening, feebly fell;
   A green and glowing light, like that which drops
From folded lilies in which glow-worms dwell,
   When Earth over her face Night's mantle wraps;
Between the severed mountains lay on high,
Over the stream, a narrow rift of sky.

40. And, ever as she went, the Image lay
   With folded wings and unawakened eyes;
And o'er its gentle countenance did play
   The busy dreams, as thick as summer flies,
Chasing the rapid smiles that would not stay,
   And drinking the warm tears, and the sweet sighs
Inhaling, which with busy murmur vain
They had aroused from that full heart and brain.

41. And over down the prone vale, like a cloud
   Upon a stream of wind, the pinnace went:

Now lingering on the pools, in which abode
   The calm and darkness of the deep content
In which they paused ; now o'er the shallow road
   Of white and dancing waters, all besprent
With sand and polished pebbles—mortal boat
In such a shallow rapid could not float.

42. And down the earthquaking cataracts, which shiver
      Their snow-like waters into golden air,
   Or under chasms unfathomable ever
      Sepulchre them, till in their rage they tear
   A subterranean portal for the river,
      It fled.   The circling sunbows did upbear
   Its fall down the hoar precipice of spray,
   Lighting it far upon its lampless way.

43. And, when the Wizard Lady would ascend
      The labyrinths of some many-winding vale
   Which to the inmost mountain upward tend,
      She called "Hermaphroditus !"—and the pale
   And heavy hue which slumber could extend
      Over its lips and eyes, as on the gale
   A rapid shadow from a slope of grass,
   Into the darkness of the stream did pass.

44. And it unfurled its heaven-coloured pinions ;
      With stars of fire spotting the stream below,
   And from above into the Sun's dominions
      Flinging a glory like the golden glow
   In which Spring clothes her emerald-wingèd
         minions,
      All interwoven with fine feathery snow,
   And moonlight splendour of intensest rime
   With which frost paints the pines in winter time.

THE WITCH OF ATLAS.

45. And then it winnowed the elysian air
    Which ever hung about that Lady bright,
  With its ethereal vans: and, speeding there,
    Like a star up the torrent of the night,
  Or a swift eagle in the morning glare
    Breasting the whirlwind with impetuous flight,
  The pinnace, oared by those enchanted wings,
  Clove the fierce streams towards their upper springs.

46. The water flashed—like sunlight, by the prow
    Of a noon-wandering meteor flung to heaven;
  The still air seemed as if its waves did flow
    In tempest down the mountains; loosely driven,
  The Lady's radiant hair streamed to and fro;
    Beneath, the billows, having vainly striven
  Indignant and impetuous, roared to feel
  The swift and steady motion of the keel.

47. Or, when the weary moon was in the wane,
    Or in the noon of interlunar night,
  The Lady Witch in visions could not chain
    Her spirit; but sailed forth under the light
  Of shooting stars, and bade extend amain
    His storm-outspeeding wings the Hermaphrodite;
  She to the austral waters took her way.
  Beyond the fabulous Thamondocana.

48. Where, like a meadow which no scythe has shaven,
    Which rain could never bend or whirlblast shake,
  With the antarctic constellations paven,
    Canopus and his crew, lay the austral lake—
  There she would build herself a windless haven,
    Out of the clouds whose moving turrets make

The bastions of the storm, when through the sky
The spirits of the tempest thundered by—

49. A haven beneath whose translucent floor
    The tremulous stars sparkled unfathomably;
And around which the solid vapours hoar,
    Based on the level waters, to the sky
Lifted their dreadful crags, and, like a shore
    Of wintry mountains, inaccessibly
Hemmed in with rifts and precipices grey,
And hanging crags, many a cove and bay.

50. And, whilst the outer lake beneath the lash
    Of the wind's scourge foamed like a wounded
        thing,
And the incessant hail with stony clash
    Ploughed up the waters, and the flagging wing
Of the roused cormorant in the lightning flash
    Looked like the wreck of some wind-wandering
Fragment of inky thunder-smoke—this haven
Was as a gem to copy heaven engraven.

51. On which that Lady played her many pranks,
    Circling the image of a shooting star
(Even as a tiger on Hydaspes' banks
    Outspeeds the antelopes which speediest are)
In her light boat; and many quips and cranks
    She played upon the water; till the car
Of the late moon, like a sick matron wan,
To journey from the misty east began.

52. And then she called out of the hollow turrets
    Of those high clouds, white, golden, and ver-
        milion,

The armies of her ministering spirits.
  In mighty legions million after million
They came, each troop emblazoning its merits
  On meteor flags; and many a proud pavilion
Of the intertexture of the atmosphere
  They pitched upon the plain of the calm mere.

53. They framed the imperial tent of their great Queen
  Of woven exhalations, underlaid
With lambent lightning-fire, as may be seen
  A dome of thin and open ivory inlaid
With crimson silk. Cressets from the serene
  Hung there, and on the water for her tread
A tapestry of fleece-like mist was strewn,
Dyed in the beams of the ascending moon.

54. And on a throne o'erlaid with starlight, caught
  Upon those wandering isles of aery dew
Which highest shoals of mountain shipwreck not,
  She sate, and heard all that had happened new
Between the earth and moon since they had brought
  The last intelligence; and now she grew
Pale as that moon lost in the watery night,
And now she wept, and now she laughed outright.

55. These were tame pleasures.—She would often climb
  The steepest ladder of the crudded rack
Up to some beakèd cape of cloud sublime,
  And like Arion on the dolphin's back
Ride singing through the shoreless air. Oft-time,
  Following the serpent lightning's winding track,
She ran upon the platforms of the wind,
And laughed to hear the fireballs roar behind.

56. And sometimes to those streams of upper air
    Which whirl the earth in its diurnal round
  She would ascend, and win the Spirits there
    To let her join their chorus.   Mortals found
  That on those days the sky was calm and fair,
    And mystic snatches of harmonious sound
  Wandered upon the earth where'er she passed,
  And happy thoughts of hope, too sweet to last.

57. But her choice sport was, in the hours of sleep,
    To glide adown old Nilus, when he threads
  Egypt and Ethiopia from the steep
    Of utmost Axumé until he spreads,
  Like a calm flock of silver-fleeced sheep,
    His waters on the plain—and crested heads
  Of cities and proud temples gleam amid,
  And many a vapour-belted pyramid—

58. By Mœris and the Marœotid lakes,
    Strewn with faint blooms like bridal-chamber floors,
  Where naked boys bridling tame water-snakes,
    Or charioteering ghastly alligators,
  Had left on the sweet waters mighty wakes
    Of those huge forms; within the brazen doors
  Of the Great Labyrinth slept both boy and beast,
  Tired with the pomp of their Osirian feast.

59. And where within the surface of the river
    The shadows of the massy temples lie,
  And never are erased, but tremble ever
    Like things which every cloud can doom to die—
  Through lotus-paven canals, and wheresoever
    The works of man pierced that serenest sky

With tombs, and towers, and fanes—'twas her
To wander in the shadow of the night.   [delight

60. With motion like the spirit of that wind
    Whose soft step deepens slumber, her light feet
Passed through the peopled haunts of humankind,
    Scattering sweet visions from her presence sweet—
Through fane and palace-court and labyrinth mined
    With many a dark and subterranean street
Under the Nile; through chambers high and deep
She passed, observing mortals in their sleep. .

61. A pleasure sweet doubtless it was to see
    Mortals subdued in all the shapes of sleep.
Here lay two sister-twins in infancy;
    There a lone youth who in his dreams did weep;
Within, two lovers linkèd innocently
    In their loose locks which over both did creep
Like ivy from one stem; and there lay calm
Old age with snow-bright hair and folded palm.

62. But other troubled forms of sleep she saw,
    Not to be mirrored in a holy song—
Distortions foul of supernatural awe,
    And pale imaginings of visioned wrong,
And all the code of Custom's lawless law
    Written upon the brows of old and young.
"This," said the Wizard Maiden, "is the strife
Which stirs the liquid surface of man's life."

63. And little did the light disturb her soul.
    We, the weak mariners of that wild lake,
Where'er its shores extend or billows roll,
    Our course unpiloted and starless make

O'er its wild surface to an unknown goal;
But she in the calm depths her way could take,
Where in bright bowers immortal forms abide
Beneath the weltering of the restless tide.

64. And she saw princes couched under the glow
Of sunlike gems; and round each temple-court
In dormitories ranged, row after row,
She saw the priests asleep—all of one sort,
For all were educated to be so.
The peasants in their huts, and in the port
The sailors she saw cradled on the waves,
And the dead lulled within their dreamless graves.

65. And all the forms in which those spirits lay
Were to her sight like the diaphanous
Veils in which those sweet ladies oft array
Their delicate limbs who would conceal from us
Only their scorn of all concealment: they
Move in the light of their own beauty thus.
But these and all now lay with sleep upon them,
And little thought a Witch was looking on them.

66. She all those human figures breathing there
Beheld as living spirits. To her eyes
The naked beauty of the soul lay bare,
And often through a rude and worn disguise
She saw the inner form most bright and fair:
And then she had a charm of strange device,
Which, murmured on mute lips with tender tone,
Could make that spirit mingle with her own.

67. Alas! Aurora, what wouldst thou have given
For such a charm, when Tithon became grey—

THE WITCH OF ATLAS.

  Or how much, Venus, of thy silver heaven
   Wouldst thou have yielded, ere Proserpina
  Had half (oh ! why not all ?) the debt forgiven
   Which dear Adonis had been doomed to pay—
  To any witch who would have taught you it ?
  The Heliad doth not know its value yet.

68. 'Tis said in after times her spirit free
   Knew what love was, and felt itself alone :
  But holy Dian could not chaster be
   Before she stooped to kiss Endymion
  Than now this Lady. Like a sexless bee,
   Tasting all blossoms and confined to none,
  Among those mortal forms the Wizard Maiden
  Passed with an eye serene and heart unladen.

69. To those she saw most beautiful she gave
   Strange panacea in a crystal bowl.
  They drank in their deep sleep of that sweet wave,
   And lived thenceforward as if some control,
  Mightier than life, were in them ; and the grave
   Of such, when death oppressed the weary soul,
  Was as a green and overarching bower
  Lit by the gems of many a starry flower.

70. For, on the night that they were buried, she
   Restored the embalmer's ruining, and shook
  The light out of the funeral lamps, to be
   A mimic day within that deathy nook ;
  And she unwound the woven imagery
   Of second childhood's swaddling bands, and took
  The coffin, its last cradle, from its niche,
  And threw it with contempt into a ditch.

71. And there the body lay, age after age,
    Mute, breathing, beating, warm, and undecaying,
Like one asleep in a green hermitage—
    With gentle sleep about its eyelids playing,
And living in its dreams beyond the rage
    Of death or life; while they were still arraying
In liveries ever new the rapid, blind,
And fleeting generations of mankind.

72. And she would write strange dreams upon the brain
    Of those who were less beautiful, and make
All harsh and crooked purposes more vain
    Than in the desert is the serpent's wake
Which the sand covers. All his evil gain
    The miser, in such dreams, would rise and shake
Into a beggar's lap; the lying scribe
Would his own lies betray without a bribe.

73. The priests would write an explanation full,
    Translating hieroglyphics into Greek,
How the god Apis really was a bull,
    And nothing more; and bid the herald stick
The same against the temple doors, and pull
    The old cant down: they licensed all to speak
Whate'er they thought of hawks, and cats, and geese,
By pastoral letters to each diocese.

74. The king would dress an ape up in his crown
    And robes, and seat him on his glorious seat,
And on the right hand of the sunlike throne
    Would place a gaudy mockbird to repeat
The chatterings of the monkey. Every one
    Of the prone courtiers crawled to kiss the feet
Of their great emperor when the morning came;
And kissed—alas, how many kiss the same!

THE WITCH OF ATLAS.

75. The soldiers dreamed that they were blacksmiths, and
    Walked out of quarters in somnambulism ;
Round the red anvils you might see them stand
    Like Cyclopses in Vulcan's sooty abysm,
Beating their swords to ploughshares : in a band
    The gaolers sent those of the liberal schism
Free through the streets of Memphis—much, I wis,
To the annoyance of king Amasis.

76. And timid lovers, who had been so coy
    They hardly knew whether they loved or not,
Would rise out of their rest, and take sweet joy,
    To the fulfilment of their inmost thought ;
And, when next day the maiden and the boy
    Met one another, both, like sinners caught,
Blushed at the thing which each believed was done
Only in fancy—till the tenth moon shone ;

77. And then the Witch would let them take no ill :
    Of many thousand schemes which lovers find,
The Witch found one—and so they took their fill
    Of happiness in marriage warm and kind.
Friends who, by practice of some envious skill,
    Were torn apart (a wide wound, mind from mind)
She did unite again with visions clear
Of deep affection and of truth sincere.

78. These were the pranks she played among the cities
    Of mortal men. And what she did to sprites
And gods, entangling them in her sweet ditties,
    To do her will, and show their subtle sleights,
I will declare another time ; for it is
    A tale more fit for the weird winter nights
Than for these garish summer days, when we
Scarcely believe much more than we can see.

POEMS WRITTEN IN 1819.

THE MASQUE OF ANARCHY.

1. AS I lay asleep in Italy,
   There came a voice from over the sea,
   And with great power it forth led me
   To walk in the visions of Poesy.

2. I met Murder on the way—
   He had a mask like Castlereagh.
   Very smooth he looked, yet grim;
   Seven bloodhounds followed him.

3. All were fat; and well they might
   Be in admirable plight,
   For one by one, and two by two,
   He tossed them human hearts to chew,
   Which from his wide cloak he drew.

4. Next came Fraud, and he had on,
   Like Lord Eldon, an ermine gown.
   His big tears, for he wept well,
   Turned into millstones as they fell;

5. And the little children who
   Round his feet played to and fro,
   Thinking every tear a gem,
   Had their brains knocked out by them.

6. Clothed with the Bible, as with light
   And the shadows of the night,
   Like Sidmouth next, Hypocrisy
   On a crocodile came by.

7. And many more Destructions played
   In this ghastly masquerade—
   All disguised, even to the eyes,
   Like bishops, lawyers, peers, or spies.

8. Last came Anarchy; he rode
   On a white horse splashed with blood;
   He was pale even to the lips,
   Like Death in the Apocalypse.

9. And he wore a kingly crown;
   In his hand a sceptre shone;
   On his brow this mark I saw—
   "I am God, and King, and Law!"

10. With a pace stately and fast
    Over English land he passed,
    Trampling to a mire of blood
    The adoring multitude.

11. And a mighty troop around
    With their trampling shook the ground,
    Waving each a bloody sword
    For the service of their lord.

12. And with glorious triumph they
    Rode through England, proud and gay,
    Drunk as with intoxication
    Of the wine of desolation.

13. O'er fields and towns, from sea to sea,
    Passed the pageant swift and free,
    Tearing up and trampling down,
    Till they came to London town.

14. And each dweller panic-stricken,
    Felt his heart with terror sicken,
    Hearing the tempestuous cry
    Of the triumph of Anarchy.

15. For with pomp to meet him came,
    Clothed in arms like blood and flame,
    The hired murderers who did sing,
    "Thou art God, and Law, and King!

16. "We have waited, weak and lone,
    For thy coming, Mighty One!
    Our purses are empty, our swords are cold;
    Give us glory, and blood, and gold."

17. Lawyers and priests, a motley crowd,
    To the earth their pale brows bowed—
    Like a bad prayer not over loud,
    Whispering "Thou art Law and God!"

18. Then all cried with one accord,
    "Thou art King, and Law, and Lord;
    Anarchy, to thee we bow,
    Be thy name made holy now!"

MASQUE OF ANARCHY.

19. And Anarchy the skeleton
    Bowed and grinned to every one
    As well as if his education
    Had cost ten millions to the nation.

20. For he knew the palaces
    Of our kings were nightly his;
    His the sceptre, crown, and globe,
    And the gold-inwoven robe.

21. So he sent his slaves before
    To seize upon the Bank and Tower,
    And was proceeding with intent
    To meet his pensioned parliament,

22. When one fled past, a maniac maid,
    And her name was Hope, she said,
    But she looked more like Despair;
    And she cried out in the air:

23. "My father Time is weak and grey
    With waiting for a better day;
    See how idiot-like he stands,
    Fumbling with his palsied hands!

24. "He has had child after child,
    And the dust of death is piled
    Over every one but me—
    Misery! oh Misery!"

25. Then she lay down in the street
    Right before the horses' feet,
    Expecting with a patient eye
    Murder, Fraud, and Anarchy—

26. When between her and her foes
   A mist, a light, an image rose,
   Small at first, and weak and frail,
   Like the vapour of the gale:

27. Till, as clouds grow on the blast,
   Like tower-crowned giants striding fast,
   And glare with lightnings as they fly,
   And speak in thunder to the sky,

28. It grew—a shape arrayed in mail
   Brighter than the viper's scale,
   And upborne on wings whose grain
   Was like the light of sunny rain.

29. On its helm seen far away
   A planet like the morning's lay;
   And those plumes its light rained through,
   Like a shower of crimson dew.

30. With step as soft as wind it passed
   O'er the heads of men: so fast
   That they knew the presence there,
   And looked—and all was empty air.

31. As flowers beneath May's footsteps waken,
   As stars from Night's loose hair are shaken,
   As waves arise when loud winds call,
   Thoughts sprung where'er that step did fall.

32. And the prostrate multitude
   Looked—and, ankle-deep in blood,
   Hope, that maiden most serene,
   Was walking with a quiet mien;

32. And Anarchy, the ghastly birth,
Lay dead earth upon the earth ;
The horse of Death, tameless as wind,
Fled, and with his hoofs did grind
To dust the murderers thronged behind.

34. A rushing light of clouds and splendour,
A sense awakening and yet tender,
Was heard and felt—and at its close
These words of joy and fear arose ;

35. As if their own indignant Earth,
Which gave the sons of England birth,
Had felt their blood upon her brow,
And, shuddering with a mother's throe,

36. Had turned every drop of blood
By which her face had been bedewed
To an accent unwithstood,
As if her heart had cried aloud.

37. "Men of England, heirs of glory,
Heroes of unwritten story,
Nurslings of one mighty mother,
Hopes of her and one another !

38. "Rise, like lions after slumber,
In unvanquishable number !
Shake your chains to earth, like dew
Which in sleep had fallen on you !

39. "What is freedom ? Ye can tell
That which Slavery is too well,
For its very name has grown
To an echo of you own.

40. "'Tis to work, and have such pay
 As just keeps life from day to day
 In your limbs as in a cell
 For the tyrants' use to dwell:

41. "So that ye for them are made
 Loom, and plough, and sword, and spade;
 With or without your own will, bent
 To their defence and nourishment.

42. "'Tis to see your children weak
 With their mothers pine and peak
 When the winter winds are bleak—
 They are dying whilst I speak.

43. "'Tis to hunger for such diet
 As the rich man in his riot
 Casts to the fat dogs that lie
 Surfeiting beneath his eye.

44. "'Tis to let the ghost of Gold
 Take from toil a thousandfold
 More than e'er his substance could
 In the tyrannies of old:

45. "Paper coin—that forgery
 Of the title-deeds which ye
 Hold to something of the worth
 Of the inheritance of Earth.

46. "'Tis to be a slave in soul,
 And to hold no strong control
 Over your own wills, but be
 All that others make of ye.

47. "And, at length, when ye complain
With a murmur weak and vain,
'Tis to see the tyrant's crew
Ride over your wives and you—
Blood is on the grass like dew!

48. "Then it is to feel revenge,
Fiercely thirsting to exchange
Blood for blood, and wrong for wrong:
Do not thus when ye are strong!

49. "Birds find rest in narrow nest,
When weary of their wingèd quest;
Beasts find fare in woody lair,
When storm and snow are in the air;

50. "Horses, oxen, have a home
When from daily toil they come;
Household dogs, when the wind roars,
Find a home within warm doors;

51. "Asses, swine, have litter spread,
And with fitting food are fed;
All things have a home but one—
Thou, O Englishman, hast none!

52. "This is Slavery!—Savage men,
Or wild beasts within a den,
Would endure not as ye do:
But such ills they never knew.

53. "What art thou, Freedom? Oh! could slaves
Answer from their living graves
This demand, tyrants would flee
Like a dream's dim imagery.

L

54. "Thou art not, as impostors say,
   A shadow soon to pass away,
   A superstition, and a name
   Echoing from the cave of Fame.

55. "For the labourer, thou art bread
   And a comely table spread,
   From his daily labour come,
   In a neat and happy home.

56. "Thou art clothes and fire and food
   For the trampled multitude.
   No—in countries that are free
   Such starvation cannot be
   As in England now we see!

57. "To the rich thou art a check;
   When his foot is on the neck
   Of his victim, thou dost make
   That he treads upon a snake.

58. "Thou art justice: ne'er for gold
   May thy righteous laws be sold
   As laws are in England; thou
   Shield'st alike the high and low.

59. "Thou art wisdom: freemen never
   Dream that God will damn for ever
   All who think those things untrue
   Of which priests make such ado.

60. "Thou art peace: never by thee
   Would blood and treasure wasted be
   As tyrants wasted them when all
   Leagued to quench thy flame in Gaul.

61. "What if English toil and blood
    Was poured forth even as a flood ?
    It availed, O Liberty,
    To dim—but not extinguish thee.

62. "Thou art love : the rich have kissed
    Thy feet, and, like him following Christ,
    Given their substance to the free,
    And through the rough world followed thee.

63. "Oh! turn their wealth to arms, and make
    War, for thy belovèd sake,
    On wealth and war and fraud ; whence they
    Drew the power which is their prey.

64. "Science, and poetry, and thought,
    Are thy lamps ; they make the lot
    Of the dwellers in a cot
    Such they curse their Maker not.

65. "Spirit, patience, gentleness,
    All that can adorn and bless,
    Art thou. Let deeds, not words, express
    Thine exceeding loveliness.

66. "Let a great assembly be
    Of the fearless and the free
    On some spot of English ground
    Where the plains stretch wide around.

67. "Let the blue sky overhead,
    The green earth on which ye tread,
    All that must eternal be
    Witness the solemnity.

68. "From the corners uttermost
Of the bounds of English coast;
From every hut, village, and town
Where those who live and suffer moan
For others' misery or their own;

69. "From the workhouse and the prison,
Where, pale as corpses newly risen,
Women, children, young and old,
Groan for pain, and weep for cold;

70. "From the haunts of daily life
Where is waged the daily strife
With common wants and common cares
Which sow the human heart with tares;

71. "Lastly, from the palaces
Where the murmur of distress
Echoes like the distant sound
Of a wind alive around—

72. "Those prison-halls of wealth and fashion,
Where some few feel such compassion,
For those who groan, and toil, and wail,
As must make their brethren pale—

73. "Ye who suffer woes untold
Or to feel or to behold
Your lost country bought and sold
With a price of blood and gold!

74. "Let a vast assembly be,
And with great solemnity
Declare with ne'er-said words that ye
Are, as God has made ye, free!

75. "Be your strong and simple words
    Keen to wound as sharpened swords,
    And wide as targes let them be,
    With their shade to cover ye.

76. "Let the tyrants pour around
    With a quick and startling sound,
    Like the loosening of a sea,
    Troops of armed emblazonry.

77. "Let the charged artillery drive,
    Till the dead air seems alive
    With the clash of clanging wheels,
    And the tramp of horses' heels.

78. "Let the fixèd bayonet
    Gleam with sharp desire to wet
    Its bright point in English blood,
    Looking keen as one for food.

79. "Let the horsemen's scimitars
    Wheel and flash, like sphereless stars
    Thirsting to eclipse their burning
    In a sea of death and mourning.

80. "Stand ye calm and resolute,
    Like a forest close and mute,
    With folded arms, and looks which are
    Weapons of an unvanquished war.

81. "And let Panic, who outspeeds
    The career of armèd steeds,
    Pass, a disregarded shade,
    Through your phalanx undismayed.

82. "Let the laws of your own land,
    Good or ill, between ye stand,
    Hand to hand, and foot to foot,
    Arbiters of the dispute—

83. "The old laws of England—they
    Whose reverend heads with age are grey,
    Children of a wiser day;
    And whose solemn voice must be
    Thine own echo—Liberty!

84. "On those who first should violate
    Such sacred heralds in their state
    Rest the blood that must ensue;
    And it will not rest on you.

85. "And, if then the tyrants dare,
    Let them ride among you there,
    Slash, and stab, and maim, and hew:
    What they like, that let them do.

86. "With folded arms and steady eyes,
    And little fear and less surprise,
    Look upon them as they slay,
    Till their rage has died away.

87. "Then they will return with shame
    To the place from which they came,
    And the blood thus shed will speak
    In hot blushes on their cheek.

88. "Every woman in the land
    Will point at them as they stand—
    They will hardly dare to greet
    Their acquaintance in the street;

89. "And the bold true warriors
   Who have hugged danger in the wars
   Will turn to those who would be free,
   Ashamed of such base company:

90. "And that slaughter to the nation
   Shall steam up like inspiration,
   Eloquent, oracular,
   A volcano heard afar:

91. "And these words shall then become
   Like Oppression's thundered doom,
   Ringing through each heart and brain,
   Heard again—again—again!

92. "Rise, like lions after slumber,
   In unvanquishable number!
   Shake your chains to earth, like dew
   Which in sleep had fallen on you!
   Ye are many—they are few?"

LINES.

WRITTEN DURING THE CASTLEREAGH ADMINISTRATION.

1. CORPSES are cold in the tomb;
   Stones on the pavement are dumb;
   Abortions are dead in the womb,
   And their mothers look pale—like the white shore
   Of Albion, free no more.

2. *Her* sons are as stones in the way—
  They are masses of senseless clay—
  They are trodden, and move not away;
 The abortion with which *she* travaileth
  Is Liberty, smitten to death.

3. Than trample and dance, thou oppressor,
  For thy victim is no redressor!
  Thou art sole lord and possessor
 Of her corpses, and clods, and abortions—they pave
  Thy path to the grave.

4. Hear'st thou the festival din
  Of Death, and Destruction, and Sin,
  And Wealth crying "Havoc!" within!
 'Tis the bacchanal triumph which makes Truth dumb,
  Thine epithalamium.

5. Ay, marry thy ghastly Wife!
  Let Fear, and Disquiet, and Strife
  Spread thy couch in the chamber of Life!
 Marry Ruin, thou tyrant! and God be thy guide
  To the bed of the bride!

SONG—TO THE MEN OF ENGLAND.

1. MEN of England, wherefore plough
   For the lords who lay you low?
 Wherefore weave with toil and care
 The rich robes your tyrants wear?

2. Wherefore feed, and clothe, and save,
From the cradle to the grave,
Those ungrateful drones who would
Drain your sweat—nay, drink your blood ?

3. Wherefore, Bees of England, forge
Many a weapon, chain, and scourge,
That these stingless drones may spoil
The forced produce of your toil ?

4. Have ye leisure, comfort, calm,
Shelter, food, love's gentle balm ?
Or what is it ye buy so dear
With your pain and with your fear ?

5. The seed ye sow another reaps ;
The wealth ye find another keeps ;
The robes ye weave another wears ;
The arms ye forge another bears.

6. Sow seed—but let no tyrant reap ;
Find wealth—let no impostor heap ;
Weave robes—let not the idle wear ;
Forge arms, in your defence to bear.

7. Shrink to your cellars, holes, and cells ;
In halls ye deck another dwells.
Why shake the chains ye wrought ? Ye see
The steel ye tempered glance on ye.

8. With plough, and spade, and hoe, and loom,
Trace your grave, and build your tomb,
And weave your winding-sheet, till fair
England be your sepulchre !

ENGLAND IN 1819.

AN old, mad, blind, despised, and dying king—
   Princes, the dregs of their dull race, who flow
Through public scorn, mud from a muddy spring,
   Rulers who neither see, nor feel, nor know,
But leech-like to their fainting country cling,
   Till they drop, blind in blood, without a blow—
A people starved and stabbed in the untilled field—
   An army which liberticide and prey
Make as a two-edged sword to all who wield—
   Golden and sanguine laws which tempt and slay—
Religion Christless, Godless, a book sealed—
A senate—time's worst statute unrepealed—
   Are graves from which a glorious Phantom may
Burst to illumine our tempestuous day.

SIMILES FOR TWO POLITICAL CHARACTERS OF 1819.

1. AS from an ancestral oak
     Two empty ravens sound their clarion,
  Yell by yell and croak by croak,
  When they scent the noonday smoke
    Of fresh human carrion :—

2. As two gibbering night-birds flit
    From their bowers of deadly hue
  Through the night to frighten it,
  When the moon is in a fit,
    And the stars are none or few—

3. As a shark and dogfish wait
    Under an Atlantic isle
For the negro-ship whose freight
Is the theme of their debate,
    Wrinkling their red gills the while—

4. Are ye, two vultures sick for battle,
    Two scorpions under one wet stone,
Two bloodless wolves whose dry throats rattle,
Two crows perched on the murrained cattle,
    Two vipers tangled into one.

GOD SAVE THE QUEEN.

1. GOD prosper, speed, and save,
    God raise from England's grave,
            Her murdered Queen!
Pave with swift victory
The steps of Liberty,
Whom Britons own to be
            Immortal Queen!

2. See, she comes throned on high
    On swift Eternity!
            God save the Queen!
Millions on millions wait,
Firm, rapid, and elate,
On her majestic state—
            God save the Queen!

3. She is Thine own pure soul
   Moulding the mighty whole.
      God save the Queen!
   She is Thine own deep love
   Rained down from heaven above.
   Wherever she rest or move,
      God save our Queen!

4. 'Wilder her enemies
   In their own dark disguise!
      God save our Queen!
   All earthly things that dare
   Her sacred name to bear,
   Strip them, as kings are, bare;
      God save the Queen!

5. Be her eternal throne
   Built in our hearts alone—
      God save the Queen!
   Let the oppressor hold
   Canopied seats of gold;
   She sits enthroned of old
      O'er our hearts Queen.

6. Lips touched by seraphim
   Breathe out the choral hymn,
      "God save the Queen!"
   Sweet as if angels sang,
   Loud as that trumpet's clang
   Wakening the world's dead gang—
      God save the Queen!

AN ODE TO THE ASSERTERS OF LIBERTY.

1. ARISE, arise, arise !
   There is blood on the earth that denies ye bread !
   Be your wounds like eyes
   To weep for the dead, the dead, the dead.
   What other grief were it just to pay ?
   Your sons, your wives, your brethren, were they !
   Who said they were slain on the battle-day ?

2. Awaken, awaken, awaken !
   The slave and the tyrant are twin-born foes.
   Be the cold chains shaken
   To the dust where your kindred repose, repose :
   Their bones in the grave will start and move
   When they hear the voices of those they love
   Most loud in the holy combat above.

3. Wave, wave high the banner
   When Freedom is riding to conquest by :
   Though the slaves that fan her
   Be Famine and Toil, giving sigh for sigh.
   And ye who attend her imperial car,
   Lift not your hands in the banded war,
   But in her defence whose children ye are.

4. Glory, glory, glory,
   To those who have greatly suffered and done !
   Never name in story
   Was greater than that which ye shall have won.

Conquerers have conquered their foes alone,
Whose revenge, pride, and power, they have over-
    thrown:
Ride ye, more victorious, over your own.

5. Bind, bind every brow
With crownals of violet, ivy, and pine:
    Hide the blood-stains now
With hues which sweet Nature has made divine—
Green strength, azure hope, and eternity.
But let not the pansy among them be;
Ye were injured, and that means memory.

ODE TO HEAVEN.

CHORUS OF SPIRITS.

FIRST SPIRIT.

PALACE-ROOF of cloudless nights!
    Paradise of golden lights!
Deep, immeasurable, vast,
    Which art now, and which wert then!
Of the present and the past,
    Of the eternal where and when,
Presence-chamber, temple, home!
Ever-canopying dome
Of acts and ages yet to come!

Glorious shapes have life in thee—
Earth, and all earth's company;
Living globes which ever throng
    Thy deep chasms and wildernesses;

ODE TO HEAVEN.

And green worlds that glide along;
   And swift stars with flashing tresses
And icy moons most cold and bright
And mighty suns beyond the night,
Atoms of intensest light.

Even thy name is as a god,
Heaven! for thou art the abode
Of that Power which is the glass
   Wherein man his nature sees.
Generations as they pass
   Worship thee with bended knees.
Their unremaining gods and they
Like a river roll away;
Thou remainest such alway.

SECOND SPIRIT.

Thou art but the mind's first chamber
Round which its young fancies clamber,
Like weak insects in a cave
   Lighted up by stalactites;
But the portal of the grave—
   Where a world of new delights
Will make thy best glories seem
But a dim and noonday gleam
From the shadow of a dream!

THIRD SPIRIT.

Peace! the abyss is wreathed with scorn
At your presumption, atom-born!
What is heaven? and what are ye
   Who its brief expanse inherit?
What are suns and spheres which flee
   With the instinct of that Spirit

Of which ye are but a part!
Drops which Nature's mighty heart
Drives through thinnest veins.   Depart!

What is heaven?   A globe of dew,
Filling in the morning new
Some eyed flower whose young leaves waken
　On an unimagined world—
Constellated suns unshaken,
　Orbits measureless, are furled
In that frail and fading sphere,
With ten millions gathered there,
To tremble, gleam, and disappear.

ODE TO THE WEST WIND.

1.　O WILD West Wind, thou breath of Autumn's
　　　being,
　Thou from whose unseen presence the leaves dead
Are driven like ghosts from an enchanter fleeing,

　Yellow, and black, and pale, and hectic red,
Pestilence-stricken multitudes: O thou
　Who chariotest to their dark wintry bed

The wingèd seeds, where they lie cold and low,
　Each like a corpse within its grave, until
Thine azure sister of the Spring shall blow

　Her clarion o'er the dreaming earth, and fill
(Driving sweet buds like flocks to feed in air)
　With living hues and odours plain and hill;

ODE TO THE WEST WIND. 177

    Wild Spirit which art moving everywhere;
Destroyer and preserver; hear, oh hear!

2. Thou on whose stream, 'mid the steep sky's com-
      motion,
  Loose clouds like earth's decaying leaves are shed,
Shook from the tangled boughs of heaven and ocean,
  Angels of rain and lightning! there are spread
On the blue surface of thine airy surge,
  Like the bright hair uplifted from the head

Of some fierce Mænad, even from the dim verge
  Of the horizon to the zenith's height,
The locks of the approaching storm. Thou dirge
  Of the dying year, to which this closing night
Will be the dome of a vast sepulchre,
  Vaulted with all thy congregated might
Of vapours, from whose solid atmosphere
Black rain, and fire, and hail, will burst: Oh hear!

3. Thou who didst waken from his summer dreams
    The blue Mediterranean, where he lay,
Lulled by the coil of his crystalline streams,

  Beside a pumice isle in Baiæ's bay,
And saw in sleep old palaces and towers
  Quivering within the wave's intenser day,
All overgrown with azure moss, and flowers
  So sweet the sense faints picturing them! Thou
For whose path the Atlantic's level powers

  Cleave themselves into chasms, while far below
The sea-blooms and the oozy woods which wear
  The sapless foliage of the ocean know

ODE TO THE WEST WIND.

Thy voice, and suddenly grow grey with fear,
And tremble and despoil themselves: Oh, hear!

4. If I were a dead leaf thou mightest bear;
    If I were a swift cloud to fly with thee;
    A wave to pant beneath thy power, and share

  The impulse of thy strength, only less free
Than thou, O uncontrollable! if even
  I were as in my boyhood, and could be

The comrade of thy wanderings over heaven,
  As then, when to outstrip thy skiey speed
Scarce seemed a vision—I would ne'er have striven

  As thus with thee in prayer in my sore need.
Oh! lift me as a wave, a leaf, a cloud!
  I fall upon the thorns of life! I bleed!

A heavy weight of hours has chained and bowed
One too like thee—tameless, and swift, and proud.

5. Make me thy lyre, even as the forest is:
    What if my leaves are falling like its own!
    The tumult of thy mighty harmonies

  Will take from both a deep autumnal tone,
Sweet though in sadness. Be thou, Spirit fierce,
  My spirit! Be thou me, impetuous one!

Drive my dead thoughts over the universe,
  Like withered leaves, to quicken a new birth;
And, by the incantation of this verse,

  Scatter, as from an unextinguished hearth
Ashes and sparks, my words among mankind!
  Be through my lips to unawakened earth

The trumpet of a prophecy! O Wind,
If Winter comes, can Spring be far behind!

AN EXHORTATION.

CHAMELEONS feed on light and air;
   Poets food is love and fame.
If in this wide world of care
   Poets could but find the same
With as little toil as they,
   Would they ever change their hue
   As the light chameleons do,
Suiting it to every ray
      Twenty times a-day ?

Poets are on this cold earth
   As chameleons might be
Hidden from their early birth
   In a cave beneath the sea.
Where light is, chameleons change;
   Where love is not, poets do.
   Fame is love disguised: if few
Find either, never think it strange
      That poets range.

Yet dare not stain with wealth or power
   A poet's free and heavenly mind.
If bright chameleons should devour
   Any food but beams and wind,
They would grow as earthly soon
   As their brother lizards are.
   Children of a sunnier star,
Spirits from beyond the moon,
      Oh! refuse the boon!

THE INDIAN SERENADE.

I ARISE from dreams of thee
  In the first sweet sleep of night,
 When the winds are breathing low,
And the stars are shining bright.
I arise from dreams of thee,
And a spirit in my feet
    Hath led me—who knows how?
    To thy chamber window sweet!

  The wandering airs they faint
    On the dark, the silent stream—
      The champak odours fail
    Like sweet thoughts in a dream;
  The nightingale's complaint
  It dies upon her heart,
    As I must die on thine,
  Belovèd as thou art!

  Oh, lift me from the grass!
    I die, I faint, I fail!
  Let thy love in kisses rain
    On my lips and eyelids pale.
My cheek is cold and white, alas!
  My heart beats loud and fast:
Oh! press it close to thine again,
  Where it will break at last.

LINES WRITTEN FOR MISS SOPHIA STACEY.

1. THOU art fair, and few are fairer
    Of the nymphs of earth or ocean.
  They are robes that fit the wearer—
    Those soft limbs of thine, whose motion
  Ever falls, and shifts, and glances,
  As the life within them dances.

2. Thy deep eyes, a double planet,
    Gaze the wisest into madness
  With soft clear fire. The winds that fan it
    Are those thoughts of gentle gladness
  Which, like zephyrs on the billow,
  Make thy gentle soul their pillow.

3. If whatever face thou paintest
    In those eyes grows pale with pleasure,
  If the fainting soul is faintest
    When it hears thy harp's wild measure,
  Wonder not that, when thou speakest,
  Of the weak my heart is weakest.

4. As dew beneath the wind of morning,
    As the sea which whirlwinds waken,
  As the birds at thunder's warning,
    As aught mute but deeply shaken,
  As one who feels an unseen spirit,
  Is my heart when thine is near it.

Via Val Fonda, Florence.

EPIPSYCHIDION:

Verses addressed to the noble and unfortunate lady,

EMILY VIVIANI,

Now imprisoned in the convent of St. Anne, Pisa.

"L'anima amante si slancia fuori del creato, e si crea nell' infinito un mondo tutto per essa, diverso assai da questo oscuro e pauroso baratro."—*Her own words.*

> My song, I fear that thou wilt find but few
> Who fitly shall conceive thy reasoning,
>   Of such hard matter dost thou entertain;
> Whence, if by misadventure chance should bring
> Thee to base company (as chance may do),
>   Quite unaware of what thou dost contain,
>   I prithee comfort thy sweet self again,
> My last delight: tell them that they are dull,
> And bid them own that thou art beautiful.

ADVERTISEMENT.

THE writer of the following lines died at Florence, as he was preparing for a voyage to one of the wildest of the Sporades, which he had bought, and where he had fitted up the ruins of an old building; and where it was his hope to have realised a scheme of life suited perhaps to that happier and better world of which he is now an inhabitant, but hardly practicable in this.

His life was singular; less on account of the romantic vicissitudes which diversified it than the ideal tinge which it received from his own character and feelings. The present poem, like the *Vita Nova* of Dante, is sufficiently intelligible to a certain class of readers without a matter-of-fact history of the circumstances to which it relates; and to a certain other class it must ever remain incomprehensible, from a defect of a common organ of preception for the ideas of which it treats. Not but that "*gran vergogna sarebbe a colui che rimasse cosa sotto veste di figura o di colore rettorico, e domandato non sapesse denudare le sue parole da cotal veste, in guisa che avessero verace intendimento.*"

The present poem appears to have been intended by the writer as the dedication to some longer one. The stanza on the preceding page is almost a literal translation from Dante's famous canzone

"*Voi che intendendo il terzo ciel movete,*" etc.

The presumptuous application of the concluding lines to his own composition will raise a smile at the expense of my unfortunate friend: be it a smile not of contempt, but pity.

EPIPSYCHIDION.

SWEET Spirit, sister of that orphan one
   Whose empire is the name thou weepest on,
In my heart's temple I suspend to thee
These votive wreaths of withered memory.
Fair captive bird, who from thy narrow cage
Pourest such music that it might assuage
The rugged hearts of those who prisoned thee,
Were they not deaf to all sweet melody—
This song shall be thy rose: its petals pale
Are dead, indeed, my adored nightingale!
But soft and fragrant is the faded blossom,
And it has no thorn left to wound thy bosom.

High spirit-wingèd heart, who dost for ever
Beat thine unfeeling bars with vain endeavour,
Till those bright plumes of thought in which arrayed
It oversoared this low and worldly shade
Lie shattered, and thy panting wounded breast
Stains with dear blood its unmaternal nest—
I weep vain tears: blood would less bitter be,
Yet poured forth gladlier could it profit thee.

Seraph of heaven, too gentle to be human,
Veiling beneath that radiant form of Woman
All that is insupportable in thee
Of light, and love, and immortality!
Sweet benediction in the eternal curse!
Veiled glory of this lampless universe!
Thou moon beyond the clouds! thou living form
Among the dead! thou star above the storm!
Thou wonder, and thou beauty, and thou terror!
Thou harmony of Nature's art! thou mirror
In whom, as in the splendour of the sun,
All shapes look glorious which thou gazest on—
Ay, even the dim words which obscure thee now
Flash lightning-like with unaccustomed glow!
I pray thee that thou blot from this sad song
All of its much mortality and wrong
With those clear drops which start like sacred dew
From the twin lights thy sweet soul darkens through,
Weeping till sorrow becomes ecstasy:
Then smile on it so that it may not die.

I never thought before my death to see
Youth's vision thus made perfect. Emily,
I love thee—though the world by no thin name
Will hide that love from its unvalued shame.

Would we two had been twins of the same mother!
Or that the name my heart lent to another
Could be a sister's bond for her and thee,
Blending two beams of one eternity!
Yet were one lawful and the other true,
These names, though dear, could paint not as is due
How beyond refuge I am thine. Ah me!
I am not thine—I am a part of thee!

Sweep lamp! my moth-like muse has burnt its wings;
Or, like a dying swan who soars and sings,
Young Love should teach Time, in his own grey style,
All that thou art. Art thou not void of guile—
A lovely soul formed to be blessed and bless—
A well of sealed and sacred happiness,
Whose waters like blithe light and music are,
Vanquishing dissonance and gloom—a star
Which moves not in the moving heavens, alone—
A smile amid dark frowns—a gentle tone
Amid rude voices—a belovèd light—
A solitude, a refuge, a delight—
A lute which those whom Love has taught to play
Make music on to soothe the roughest day,
And lull fond Grief asleep—a buried treasure—
A cradle of young thoughts of wingless pleasure—
A violet-shrouded grave of woe?—I measure
The world of fancies seeking one like thee,
And find—alas! mine own infirmity.

She met me, Stranger, upon life's rough way,
And lured me towards sweet death; as Night by Day,
Winter by Spring, or Sorrow by swift Hope,
Led into light, life, peace. An antelope
In the suspended impulse of its lightness

Were less ethereally light. The brightness
Of her divinest presence trembles through
Her limbs, as underneath a cloud of dew
Embodied in the windless heaven of June,
Amid the splendour-wingèd stars, the moon
Burns inextinguishably beautiful:
And from her lips as from a hyacinth full
Of honey-dew, a liquid murmur drops,
Killing the sense with passion, sweet as stops
Of planetary music heard in trance.
In her mild lights the starry spirits dance,
The sunbeams of those wells which ever leap
Under the lightnings of the soul—too deep
For the brief fathom-line of thought or sense.

The glory of her being, issuing thence,
Stains the dead blank cold air with a warm shade
Of unentangled intermixture, made,
By Love, of light and motion; one intense
Diffusion, one serene omnipresence,
Whose flowing outlines mingle in their flowing,
Around her cheeks and utmost fingers glowing
With the unintermitted blood, which there
Quivers (as in a fleece of snow-like air
The crimson pulse of living Morn may quiver),
Continuously prolonged and ending never,
Till they are lost, and in that beauty furled
Which penetrates, and clasps, and fills the world;
Scarce visible from extreme loveliness.
Warm fragrance seems to fall from her light dress,
And her loose hair; and, where some heavy tress
The air of her own speed has disentwined,
The sweetness seems to satiate the faint wind;
And in the soul a wild odour is felt,

Beyond the sense, like fiery dews that melt
Into the bosom of a frozen bud.
See where she stands ! a mortal shape indued
With love, and life, and light, and deity,
And motion which may change but cannot die ;
An image of some bright eternity ;
A shadow of some golden dream ; a splendour
Leaving the third sphere pilotless ; a tender
Reflection of the eternal moon of love
Under whose motions life's dull billows move ;
A metaphor of Spring, and youth, and morning ;
A vision like incarnate April, warning
With smiles and tears Frost the anatomy
Into his summer grave.
                        Ah ! woe is me !
What have I dared ? where am I lifted ? how
Shall I descend, and perish not ? I know
That love makes all things equal: I have heard
By mine own heart this joyous truth averred—
The spirit of the worm beneath the sod,
In love and worship, blends itself with God.

Spouse ! sister ! angel ! pilot of the fate
Whose course has been so starless ! O too late
Beloved, O too soon adored, by me !
For in the fields of immortality
My spirit should at first have worshipped thine,
A divine presence in a place divine ;
Or should have moved beside it on this earth,
A shadow of that substance, from its birth :
But not as now.—I love thee ; yes, I feel
That on the fountain of my heart a seal
Is set, to keep its waters pure and bright
For thee, since in those tears thou hast delight.

We—are we not formed, as notes of music are,
For one another, though dissimilar?
Such difference without discord as can make
Those sweetest sounds in which all spirits shake,
As trembling leaves in a continuous air.

Thy wisdom speaks in me, and bids me dare
Beacon the rocks on which high hearts are wrecked.
I never was attached to that great sect
Whose doctrine is that each one should select
Out of the crowd a mistress or a friend,
And all the rest, though fair and wise, commend
To cold oblivion; though it is in the code
Of modern morals, and the beaten road
Which those poor slaves with weary footsteps tread
Who travel to their home among the dead
By the broad highway of the world, and so
With one chained friend, perhaps a jealous foe,
The dreariest and the longest journey go.

True love in this differs from gold and clay,
That to divide is not to take away.
Love is like understanding, that grows bright,
Gazing on many truths; 'tis like thy light,
Imagination, which from earth and sky,
And from the depths of human fantasy,
As from a thousand prisms and mirrors, fills
The universe with glorious beams, and kills
Error the worm with many a sunlike arrow
Of its reverberated lightning. Narrow
The heart that loves, the brain that contemplates,
The life that wears, the spirit that creates,
One object and one form, and builds thereby
A sepulchre for its eternity!

Mind from its object differs most in this:
Evil from good; misery from happiness;
The baser from the nobler; the impure
And frail from what is clear and must endure.
If you divide suffering or dross, you may
Diminish till it is consumed away;
If you divide pleasure, and love, and thought,
Each part exceeds the whole; and we know not
How much, while any yet remains unshared,
Of pleasure may be gained, of sorrow spared.
This truth is that deep well whence sages draw
The unenvied light of hope; the eternal law
By which those live to whom this world of life
Is as a garden ravaged, and whose strife
Tills for the promise of a later birth
The wilderness of this elysian earth.

There was a Being whom my spirit oft
Met on its visioned wanderings, far aloft,
In the clear golden prime of my youth's dawn,
Upon the fairy isles of sunny lawn,
Amid the enchanted mountains, and the caves
Of divine sleep, and on the air-like waves
Of wonder-level dream, whose tremulous floor
Paved her light steps. On an imagined shore,
Under the grey beak of some promontory,
She met me, robed in such exceeding glory
That I beheld her not. In solitudes
Her voice came to me through the whispering woods,
And from the fountains, and the odours deep
Of flowers, which, like lips murmuring in their sleep
Of the sweet kisses which had lulled them there,
Breathed but of her to the enamoured air;
And from the breezes whether low or loud,

And from the rain of every passing cloud,
And from the singing of the summer birds,
And from all sounds, all silence. In the words
Of antique verse and high romance—in form,
Sound, colour—in whatever checks that storm
Which with the shattered present chokes the past—
And in that best philosophy whose taste
Makes this cold common hell, our life, a doom
As glorious as a fiery martyrdom—
Her Spirit was the harmony of truth.

Then from the caverns of my dreamy youth
I sprang, as one sandalled with plumes of fire,
And towards the lodestar of my own desire
I flitted, like a dizzy moth whose flight
Is as a dead leaf's in the owlet light,
When it would seek in Hesper's setting sphere
A radiant death, a fiery sepulchre,
As if it were a lamp of earthly flame.
But she, whom prayers or tears then could not tame,
Passed, like a god throned on a wingèd planet,
Whose burning plumes to tenfold swiftness fan it,
Into the dreary cone of our life's shade.
And, as a man with mighty loss dismayed,
I would have followed, though the grave between
Yawned like a gulf whose spectres are unseen :
When a voice said, "O thou of hearts the weakest,
The phantom is beside thee whom thou seekest."
Then I—"Where ?" The world's echo answered,
  "Where ?"
And in that silence and in my despair
I questioned every tongueless wind that flew
Over my tower of mourning, if it knew
Whither 'twas fled, this soul out of my soul ;

And murmured names and spells which have control
Over the sightless tyrants of our fate.
But neither prayer nor verse could dissipate
The night which closed on her; nor uncreate
That world within this chaos, mine and me,
Of which she was the veiled divinity—
The world, I say, of thoughts that worshipped her.
And therefore I went forth—with hope, and fear,
And every gentle passion, sick to death,
Feeding my course with expectation's breath—
Into the wintry forest of our life;
And, struggling through its error with vain strife,
And stumbling in my weakness and my haste,
And half bewildered by new forms, I passed,
Seeking among those untaught foresters
If I could find one form, resembling hers,
In which she might have masked herself from me.
There, one whose voice was venomed melody
Sate by a well, under blue nightshade bowers.
The breath of her false mouth was like faint flowers;
Her touch was as electric poison; flame
Out of her looks into my vitals came;
And from her living cheeks and bosom flew
A killing air which pierced like honey-dew
Into the core of my green heart, and lay
Upon its leaves—until, as hair grown grey
O'er a young brow, they hid its unblown prime
With ruins of unseasonable time.

In many mortal forms I rashly sought
The shadow of that idol of my thought.
And some were fair—but beauty dies away:
Others were wise—but honeyed words betray:
And one was true—oh! why not true to me!

Then, as a hunted deer that could not flee,
I turned upon my thoughts, and stood at bay,
Wounded, and weak, and panting; the cold day
Trembled for pity of my strife and pain—
When, like a noonday dawn, there shone again
Deliverance. One stood on my path who seemed
As like the glorious shape which I had dreamed
As is the Moon, whose changes ever run
Into themselves, to the eternal Sun;
The cold chaste Moon, the queen of heaven's bright
    isles,
Who makes all beautiful on which she smiles—
That wandering shrine of soft yet icy flame
Which ever is transformed yet still the same,
And warms not; but illumines. Young and fair
As the descended Spirit of that sphere
She hid me, as the Moon may hide the Night
From its own darkness, until all was bright
Between the heaven and earth of my calm mind;
And, as a cloud charioted by the wind,
She led me to a cave in that wild place,
And sat beside me, with her downward face
Illumining my slumbers, like the Moon
Waxing and waning o'er Endymion.
And I was laid asleep, spirit and limb,
And all my being became bright or dim
As the Moon's image in a summer sea,
According as she smiled or frowned on me;
And there I lay within a chaste cold bed.
Alas! I then was nor alive nor dead—
For at her silver voice came Death and Life,
Unmindful each of their accustomed strife,
Masked like twin babes, a sister and a brother,
The wandering hopes of one abandoned mother:

And through the cavern without wings they flew,
And cried, "Away! he is not of our crew."
I wept; and, though it be a dream, I weep.

What storms then shook the ocean of my sleep,
Blotting that Moon whose pale and waning lips
Then shrank as in the sickness of eclipse;
And how my soul was as a lampless sea,
And who was then its tempest; and, when she,
The planet of that hour, was quenched, what frost
Crept o'er those waters, till from coast to coast
The moving billows of my being fell
Into a death of ice, immovable;
And then what earthquakes made it gape and split,
The white Moon smiling all the while on it—
These words conceal. If not, each word would be
The key of staunchless tears. Weep not for me!

At length, into the obscure forest came
The vision I had sought through grief and shame.
Athwart that wintry wilderness of thorns
Flashed from her motion splendour like the morn's,
And from her presence life was radiated
Through the grey earth and branches bare and dead;
So that her way was paved and roofed above
With flowers as soft as thoughts of budding love;
And music from her respiration spread
Like light—all other sounds were penetrated
By the small, still, sweet spirit of that sound,
So that the savage winds hung mute around;
And odours warm and fresh fell from her hair,
Dissolving the dull cold in the frore air.
Soft as an incarnation of the Sun,
When light is changed to love, this glorious one

Floated into the cavern where I lay,
And called my spirit; and the dreaming clay
Was lifted by the thing that dreamed below
As smoke by fire, and in her beauty's glow
I stood, and felt the dawn of my long night
Was penetrating me with living light.
I knew it was the Vision veiled from me
So many years—that it was Emily.

Twin spheres of light who rule this passive earth,
This world of love, this *me;* and into birth
Awaken all its fruits and flowers, and dart
Magnetic might into its central heart;
And lift its billows and its mists, and guide
By everlasting laws each wind and tide
To its fit cloud and its appointed cave;
And lull its storms, each in the craggy grave
Which was its cradle, luring to faint bowers
The armies of the rainbow-wingèd showers;
And, as those married lights which from the towers
Of heaven look forth, and fold the wandering globe
In liquid sleep and splendour as a robe,
And all their many-mingled influence blend,
If equal yet unlike, to one sweet end,
So ye, bright regents, with alternate sway,
Govern my sphere of being, night and day—
Thou, not disdaining even a borrowed might,
Thou, not eclipsing a remoter light—
And through the shadow of the seasons three,
From Spring to Autumn's sere maturity,
Light it into the winter of the tomb,
Where it may ripen to a brighter bloom!—
Thou too, O Comet, beautiful and fierce,
Who drew'st the heart of this frail universe

Towards thine own ; till wrecked in that convulsion,
Alternating attraction and repulsion,
Thine went astray, and that was rent in twain ;
Oh ! float into our azure heaven again !
Be there love's folding-star at thy return !
The living Sun will feed thee from its urn
Of golden fire ; the Moon will veil her horn
In thy last smiles ; adoring Even and Morn
Will worship thee with incense of calm breath
And lights and shadows, as the star of death
And birth is worshipped by those sisters wild
Called Hope and Fear. Upon the heart are piled
Their offerings—of this sacrifice divine
A world shall be the altar.

       Lady mine,
Scorn not these flowers of thought, the fading birth
Which from its heart of hearts that plant puts forth
Whose fruit, made perfect by thy sunny eyes,
Will be as of the trees of paradise.
The day is come, and thou wilt fly with me !
To whatsoe'er of dull mortality
Is mine remain a vestal sister still ;
To the intense, the deep, the imperishable—
Not mine, but me—henceforth be thou united,
Even as a bride, delighting and delighted.
The hour is come—the destined star has risen
Which shall descend upon a vacant prison.
The walls are high, the gates are strong, thick set
The sentinels—but true Love never yet
Was thus constrained. It overleaps all fence :
Like lightning, with invisible violence
Piercing its continents ; like heaven's free breath,
Which he who grasps can hold not ; liker Death,

Who rides upon a thought, and makes his way
Through temple, tower, and palace, and the array
Of arms.   More strength has Love than he or they;
For he can burst *his* charnel, and make free
The limbs in chains, the heart in agony,
The soul in dust and chaos.

        Emily,
A ship is floating in the harbour now,
A wind is hovering o'er the mountain's brow.
There is a path on the sea's azure floor—
No keel has ever ploughed that path before;
The halcyons brood around the foamless isles:
The treacherous ocean has foresworn its wiles;
The merry mariners are bold and free:
Say, my heart's sister, wilt thou sail with me?
Our bark is as an albatross whose nest
Is a far Eden of the purple east;
And we between her wings will sit, while Night,
And Day, and Storm, and Calm pursue their flight,
Our ministers, along the boundless sea,
Treading each other's heels, unheededly.
It is an isle under Ionian skies,
Beautiful as a wreck of paradise;
And, for the harbours are not safe and good,
This land would have remained a solitude
But for some pastoral people native there,
Who from the elysian, clear, and golden air
Draw the last spirit of the age of gold—
Simple and spirited, innocent and bold.
The blue Ægean girds this chosen home,
With ever-changing sound, and light, and foam,
Kissing the sifted sands and caverns hoar;
And all the winds wandering along the shore

Undulate with the undulating tide.
There are thick woods where sylvan forms abide;
And many a fountain, rivulet, and pond,
As clear as elemental diamond,
Or serene morning air. And far beyond,
The mossy tracks made by the goats and deer
(Which the rough shepherd treads but once a-year)
Pierce into glades, caverns, and bowers, and halls
Built round with ivy, which the waterfalls
Illumining, with sound that never fails,
Accompany the noonday nightingales.
And all the place is peopled with sweet airs;
The light clear element which the isle wears
Is heavy with the scent of lemon-flowers,
Which floats like mist laden with unseen showers,
And falls upon the eyelids like faint sleep;
And from the moss violets and jonquils peep,
And dart their arrowy odour through the brain,
Till you might faint with that delicious pain.
And every motion, odour, beam, and tone,
With that deep music is in unison
Which is a soul within the soul; they seem
Like echoes of an antenatal dream.
It is an isle 'twixt heaven, air, earth, and sea,
Cradled, and hung in clear tranquillity;
Bright as that wandering Eden, Lucifer,
Washed by the soft blue oceans of young air.
It is a favoured place. Famine or blight,
Pestilence, war, and earthquake never light
Upon its mountain-peaks; blind vultures, they
Sail onward far upon their fatal way.
The wingèd storms, chanting their thunder-psalm
To other lands, leave azure chasms of calm .
Over this isle, or weep themselves in dew,

From which its fields and woods ever renew
Their green and golden immortality.
And from the sea there rise, and from the sky
There fall, clear exhalations, soft and bright,
Veil after veil, each hiding some delight :
Which sun, or moon, or zephyr draws aside,
Till the isle's beauty, like a naked bride
Glowing at once with love and loveliness,
Blushes and trembles at its own excess.
Yet, like a buried lamp, a soul no less
Burns in the heart of this delicious isle,
An atom of the Eternal, whose own smile
Unfolds itself, and may be felt, not seen,
O'er the grey rocks, blue waves, and forests green,
Filling their bare and void interstices.

But the chief marvel of the wilderness
Is a lone dwelling, built by whom or how
None of the rustic island-people know.
'Tis not a tower of strength, though with its height
It overtops the woods ; but, for delight,
Some wise and tender Ocean-king, ere crime
Had been invented, in the world's young prime,
Reared it, a wonder of that simple time,
And envy of the isles—a pleasure-house
Made sacred to his sister and his spouse.
It scarce seems now a wreck of human art,
But, as it were, Titanic ; in the heart
Of earth having assumed its form, then grown
Out of the mountains, from the living stone
Lifting itself in caverns light and high :
For all the antique and learned imagery
Has been erased, and in the place of it
The ivy and the wild vine interknit

The volumes of their many-twining stems.
Parasite flowers illume with dewy gems
The lampless halls; and, when they fade, the sky
Peeps through their winter-woof of tracery
With moonlight patches or star atoms keen,
Or fragments of the day's intense serene,
Working mosaic on their Parian floors.
And, day and night, aloof, from the high towers
And terraces, the Earth and Ocean seem
To sleep in one another's arms, and dream
Of waves, flowers, clouds, woods, rocks, and all that
    we
Read in their smiles, and call reality.

This isle and house are mine, and I have vowed
Thee to be lady of the solitude.
And I have fitted up some chambers there
Looking towards the golden eastern air,
And level with the living winds which flow
Like waves above the living waves below.
I have sent books and music there, and all
Those instruments with which high spirits call
The future from its cradle, and the past
Out of its grave, and make the present last
In thoughts and joys which sleep but cannot die,
Folded within their own eternity.
Our simple life wants little, and true taste
Hires not the pale drudge Luxury to waste
The scene it would adorn; and therefore still
Nature with all her children haunts the hill.
The ringdove in the embowering ivy yet
Keeps up her love-lament; and the owls flit
Round the evening tower; and the young stars glance
Between the quick bats in their twilight dance;

The spotted deer bask in the fresh moonlight
Before our gate; and the slow silent night
Is measured by the pants of their calm sleep.
Be this our home in life; and, when years heap
Their withered hours like leaves on our decay,
Let us become the overhanging day,
The living soul, of this elysian isle—
Conscious, inseparable, one.   Meanwhile
We two will rise, and sit, and walk together
Under the roof of blue Ionian weather;
And wander in the meadows; or ascend
The mossy mountains, where the blue heavens bend
With lightest winds to touch their paramour;
Or linger where the pebble-paven shore
Under the quick faint kisses of the sea
Trembles and sparkles as with ecstasy—
Possessing and possessed by all that is
Within that calm circumference of bliss,
And by each other, till to love and live
Be one; or at the noontide hour arrive
Where some old cavern hoar seems yet to keep
The moonlight of the expired Night asleep,
Through which the awakened Day can never peep;
A veil for our seclusion, close as Night's,
Where secure sleep may kill thine innocent lights—
Sleep, the fresh dew of languid love, the rain
Whose drops quench kisses till they burn again.
And we will talk, until thought's melody
Become too sweet for utterance, and it die
In words, to live again in looks, which dart
With thrilling tone into the voiceless heart,
Harmonising silence without a sound.
Our breath shall intermix, our bosoms bound,
And our veins beat together; and our lips,

With other eloquence than words, eclipse
The soul that burns between them ; and the wells
Which boil under our being's inmost cells,
The fountains of our deepest life, shall be
Confused in passion's golden purity,
As mountain-springs under the morning sun.
We shall become the same, we shall be one
Spirit within two frames, oh, wherefore two ?
One passion in twin hearts, which grows and grew
Till, like two meteors of expanding flame,
Those spheres instinct with it become the same,
Touch, mingle, are transfigured ; ever still
Burning, yet ever inconsumable ;
In one another's substance finding food,
Like flames too pure, and light, and unimbued
To nourish their bright lives with baser prey,
Which point to heaven and cannot pass away :
One hope within two wills, one will beneath
Two overshadowing minds, one life, one death,
One heaven, one hell, one immortality,
And one annihilation !

     Woe is me !
The wingèd words on which my soul would pierce
Into the height of Love's rare universe
Are chains of lead around its flight of fire—
I pant, I sink, I tremble, I expire !

Weak verses, go, kneel at your Sovereign's feet,
 And say—" We are the masters of thy slave ;
  What wouldest thou with us and ours and thine ?"
Then call your sisters from Oblivion's cave,

All singing loud: "Love's very pain is sweet;
  But its reward is in the world divine,
Which, if not here, it builds beyond the grave."
  So shall ye live when I am there.   Then haste
Over the hearts of men, until ye meet
  Marina, Vanna, Primus, and the rest,
  And bid them love each other, and be blessed:
And leave the troop which errs and which reproves,
And come and be my guest—for I am Love's.

POEMS WRITTEN IN 1820.

LOVE'S PHILOSOPHY.

THE fountains mingle with the river
    And the rivers with the ocean;
The winds of heaven mix for ever
    With a sweet emotion;
Nothing in the world is single;
    All things by a law divine
In one another's being mingle—
    Why not I with thine?

See, the mountains kiss high heaven,
    And the waves clasp one another;
No sister flower would be forgiven
    If it disdained its brother;
And the sunlight clasps the earth,
    And the moonbeams kiss the sea—
What are all these kissings worth,
    If thou kiss not me?

January 1820.

ODE TO LIBERTY.

"Yet, Freedom, yet, thy banner, torn but flying,
Streams like a thunder-storm against the wind."—BYRON.

1. A GLORIOUS people vibrated again
        The lightning of the nations : Liberty,
    From heart to heart, from tower to tower, o'er Spain,
        Scattering contagious fire into the sky,
    Gleamed. My soul spurned the chains of its dismay,
            And in the rapid plumes of song
            Clothed itself, sublime and strong,
    As a young eagle soars the morning clouds among,
        Hovering inverse o'er its accustomed prey :
            Till from its station in the heaven of Fame
        The Spirit's whirlwind rapt it ; and the ray
            Of the remotest sphere of living flame
    Which paves the void was from behind it flung,
        As foam from a ship's swiftness, when there came
    A voice out of the deep ; I will record the same.

2. "The sun and the serenest moon sprang forth ;
        The burning stars of the abyss were hurled
    Into the depths of heaven ; the dædal earth,
        That island in the ocean of the world,
    Hung in its cloud of all-sustaining air.
            But this divinest universe
            Was yet a chaos and a curse,
    For Thou wert not : but, power from worst producing
            worse,
    The spirit of the beasts was kindled there,
        And of the birds, and of the watery forms—
    And there was war among them, and despair
        Within them, raging without truce or terms.

The bosom of their violated nurse
    Groaned, for beasts warred on beasts, and worms
        on worms,
And men on men ; each heart was as a hell of storms.

3. "Man, the imperial shape, then multiplied
    His generations under the pavilion
Of the sun's throne : palace and pyramid,
    Temple and prison, to many a swarming million
Were as to mountain-wolves their rugged caves.
    This human living multitude
        Was savage, cunning, blind, and rude—
For Thou wert not ; but o'er the populous solitude,
    Like one fierce cloud over a waste of waves,
        Hung Tyranny ; beneath sate deified
The Sister-pest, congregator of slaves
    Into the shadow of her pinions wide.
Anarchs and priests, who feed on gold and blood
    Till with the stain their inmost souls are dyed,
Drove the astonished herds of men from every side.

4. "The nodding promontories and blue isles
        And cloud-like mountains and dividuous waves
Of Greece basked glorious in the open smiles
    Of favouring heaven : from their enchanted caves
Prophetic echoes flung dim melody
    On the unapprehensive wild.
        The vine, the corn, the olive mild,
Grew, savage yet, to human use unreconciled ;
    And, like unfolded flowers beneath the sea,
Like the man's thought dark in the infant's brain,
    Like aught that is which wraps what is to be,
        Art's deathless dreams lay veiled by many a vein
Of Parian stone : and, yet a speechless child,

Verse murmured, and Philosophy did strain
Her lidless eyes for Thee—when ,o'er the Ægean main.

5. "Athens arose: a city such as vision
 Builds from the purple crags and silver towers
Of battlemented cloud, as in derision
 Of kingliest masonry: the ocean floors
Pave it; the evening sky pavilions it;
 Its portals are inhabited
 By thunder-zonèd winds, each head
Within its cloudy wings with sun-fire garlanded,
 A divine work! Athens diviner yet
 Gleamed with its crest of columns, on the will
Of man as on a mount of diamond set;
 For Thou wert, and thine all-creative skill
Peopled, with forms that mock the eternal dead
 In marble immortality, that hill
Which was thine earliest throne and latest oracle.

6. "Within the surface of time's fleeting river
 Its wrinkled image lies, as then it lay,
Immovably unquiet, and for ever
 It trembles, but it cannot pass away.
The voice of thy bards and sages thunder
 With an earth-awakening blast
 Through the caverns of the past;
Religion veils her eyes, Oppression shrinks aghast;
 A wingèd sound of joy, and love, and wonder,
 Which soars where expectation never flew,
Rending the veil of space and time asunder.
 One ocean feeds the clouds, and streams, and dew;
 One sun illumines heaven; one Spirit vast
 With life and love makes chaos ever new—
As Athens doth the world with thy delight renew.

ODE TO LIBERTY.

7. "Then Rome was, and from thy deep bosom fairest,
    Like a wolf-cub from a Cadmean Mænad,
   She drew the milk of greatness, though thy dearest
    From that elysian food was yet unweaned;
   And many a deed of terrible uprightness
        By thy sweet love was sanctified;
        And in thy smile and by thy side
   Saintly Camillus lived, and firm Attilius died.
    But, when tears stained thy robe of vesta
            whiteness,
        And gold profaned thy capitolian throne,
     Thou didst desert, with spirit-wingèd lightness,
        The senate of the tyrants: they sunk prone,
     Slaves of one tyrant. Palatinus sighed
        Faint echoes of Ionian song; that tone
   Thou didst delay to hear, lamenting to disown.

8. "From what Hyrcanian glen or frozen hill,
        Or piny promontory of the Arctic main,
     Or utmost islet inaccessible,
        Didst thou lament the ruin of thy reign,
     Teaching the woods and waves, and desert rocks,
        And every Naiad's ice-cold urn,
        To talk in echoes sad and stern
   Of that sublimest lore which man had dared unlearn?
     For neither didst thou watch the wizard flocks
        Of the Scald's dreams, nor haunt the Druid's
            sleep.
     What if the tears rained through thy shattered locks
        Were quickly dried? for thou didst groan, not
            weep,
     When from its sea of death, to kill and burn,
        The Galilean serpent forth did creep,
   And made thy world an undistinguishable heap.

9. "A thousand years the Earth cried, 'Where art
         thou?'
    And then the shadow of thy coming fell
    On Saxon Alfred's olive-cinctured brow :
    And many a warrior-peopled citadel,
    Like rocks which fire lifts out of the flat deep,
         Arose in sacred Italy,
         Frowning o'er the tempestuous sea
Of kings, and priests, and slaves, in tower-crowned
         majesty.
    That multitudinous anarchy did sweep
    And burst around their walls like idle foam,
Whilst from the human spirit's deepest deep
    Strange melody with love and awe struck dumb
Dissonant arms ; and Art, which cannot die,
    With divine wand traced on our earthly home
Fit imagery to pave heaven's everlasting dome.

10. "Thou Huntress swifter than the Moon! thou terror
    Of the world's wolves! thou bearer of the quiver
Whose sunlike shafts pierce tempest-wingèd Error,
    As light may pierce the clouds when they dissever
    In the calm regions of the orient day!
         Luther caught thy wakening glance:
         Like lightning from his leaden lance
Reflected, it dissolved the visions of the trance
    In which, as in a tomb, the nations lay ;
    And England's prophets hailed thee as their
         queen,
    In songs whose music cannot pass away
    Though it must flow for ever. Not unseen,
Before the spirit-sighted countenance
    Of Milton, didst thou pass from the sad scene
Beyond whose night he saw, with a dejected mien.

ODE TO LIBERTY.

11. "The eager Hours and unreluctant Years
    As on a dawn-illumined mountain stood,
Trampling to silence their loud hopes and fears,
    Darkening each other with their multitude—
And cried aloud, 'Liberty!' Indignation
        Answered Pity from her cave;
        Death grew pale within the grave,
And Desolation howled to the destroyer, 'Save!'
When, like heaven's sun girt by the exhalation
    Of its own glorious light, thou didst arise,
Chasing thy foes from nation unto nation
    Like shadows: as if day had cloven the skies
At dreaming midnight o'er the western wave,
    Men started, staggering with a glad surprise,
Under the lightnings of thine unfamiliar eyes.

12. "Thou heaven of earth! what spells could pall thee then
    In ominous eclipse? A thousand years
Bred from the slime of deep Oppression's den
    Dyed all thy liquid light with blood and tears,
Till thy sweet stars could weep the stain away.
        How, like Bacchanals of blood,
        Round France, the ghastly vintage, stood
Destruction's sceptred slaves, and Folly's mitred brood!
When one, like them, but mightier far than they,
    The Anarch of thine own bewildered powers,
Rose: armies mingled in obscure array,   [bowers
    Like clouds with clouds darkening the sacred
Of serene heaven. He, by the past pursued,
    Rests with those dead but unforgotten hours
Whose ghosts scare victor kings in their ancestral towers.

13. "England yet sleeps: was she not called of old?
　　Spain calls her now—as with its thrilling thunder
　Vesuvius wakens Ætna, and the cold
　　Snow-crags by its reply are cloven in sunder:
　O'er the lit waves every Æolian isle
　　　From Pitbecusa to Pelorus
　　　Howls, and leaps, and glares in chorus:
　They cry, 'Be dim, ye lamps of heaven suspended
　　　o'er us!'
　Her chains are threads of gold—she need but smile,
　　And they dissolve; but Spain's were links of steel,
　Till bit to dust by virtue's keenest file.
　　Twins of a single destiny! appeal
　To the eternal years enthroned before us
　　In the dim West! Impress us from a seal,
　All ye have thought and done! Time cannot dare conceal.

14. "Tomb of Arminius! render up thy dead—
　　Till, like a standard from a watch-tower's staff,
　His soul may stream over the tyrant's head!
　　Thy victory shall be his epitaph!
　Wild Bacchanal of truth's mysterious wine,
　　　King-deluded Germany,
　　　His dead spirit lives in thee!
　Why do we fear or hope? Thou art already free!—
　And thou, lost paradise of this divine
　　And glorious world! thou flowery wilderness!
　Thou island of eternity! thou shrine
　　Where Desolation, clothed with loveliness,
　Worships the thing thou wert! O Italy,
　　Gather thy blood into thy heart; repress
　The beasts who make their dens thy sacred palaces!

ODE TO LIBERTY.

15. "Oh that the free would stamp the impious name
   Of 'King' into the dust ; or write it *there*,
  So that this blot upon the page of fame
   Were as a serpent's path which the light air
  Erases, and the flat sands close behind !
     Ye the oracle have heard :
     Lift the victory-flashing sword,
  And cut the snaky knots of this foul gordian word,
   Which, weak itself as stubble, yet can bind
    Into a mass irrefragably firm
  The axes and the rods which awe mankind.
    The sound has poison in it ; 'tis the sperm
  Of what makes life foul, cankerous, and abhorred.
    Disdain not Thou, at thine appointed term,
  To set thine armèd heel on this reluctant worm.

16. "Oh that the wise from their bright minds would kindle
   Such lamps within the dome of this dim world
  That the pale name of Priest might shrink and dwindle
   Into the hell from which it first was hurled,
  A scoff of impious pride from fiends impure !
     Till human thoughts might kneel alone,
     Each before the judgment-throne
  Of its own aweless soul, or of the Power unknown.
   Oh that the words which make the thoughts obscure
    From which they spring, as clouds of glimmering dew
   From a white lake blot heaven's blue portraiture,
    Were stripped of their thin masks and various hue,
   And frowns and smiles and splendours not their own,
     Till in the nakedness of false and true
  They stand before their lord, each to receive its due !

17. "He who taught man to vanquish whatsoever
    Can be between the cradle and the grave
  Crowned him the King of Life. Oh vain endeavour.
    If on his own high will, a willing slave,
  He has enthroned the oppression and the oppressor!
        What if earth can clothe and feed
        Amplest millions at their need,
  And power in thought be as the tree within the seed—
    Or what if Art, an ardent intercessor,
      Diving on fiery wings to Nature's throne,
  Checks the great Mother stooping to caress her,
    And cries, 'Give me, thy child, dominion
  Over all height and depth'—if Life can breed
      New wants, and Wealth, from those who toil and
        groan
  Rend, of thy gifts and hers, a thousandfold for one!

18. "Come Thou! But lead out of the inmost cave
      Of man's deep spirit—as the morning star
  Beckons the Sun from the Eoan wave—
      Wisdom. I hear the pennons of her car,
  Self-moving, like cloud charioted by flame!
          Comes she not? And come ye not,
          Rulers of Eternal thought,
  To judge with solemn truth Life's ill-apportioned lot—
      Blind Love, and equal Justice, and the Fame
  Of what has been, the Hope of what will be!
    O Liberty—(if such could be thy name
        Wert thou disjoined from these, or they from
          thee)—
    If thine or theirs were treasures to be bought
        By blood or tears, have not the wise and free
  Wept tears, and blood like tears?"—The solemn
          harmony

19. Paused, and the Spirit of that mighty singing
    To its abyss was suddenly withdrawn.
Then, as a wild swan, when sublimely winging
    Its path athwart the thunder-smoke of dawn,
Sinks headlong through the aërial golden light
        On the heavy-sounding plain,
      When the bolt has pierced its brain ;
As summer clouds dissolve unburthened of their rain ;
    As a far taper fades with fading night ;
    As a brief insect dies with dying day ;
My song, its pinions disarrayed of might,
    Drooped. O'er it closed the echoes far away
Of the great voice which did its flight sustain—
    As waves which lately paved his watery way
Hiss round a drowner's head in their tempestuous play.

ARETHUSA.

1.   ARETHUSA arose
        From her couch of snows
In the Acroceraunian mountains—
    From cloud and from crag,
    With many a jag,
Shepherding her bright fountains.
    She leapt down the rocks,
    With her rainbow locks
Streaming among the streams ;
    Her steps paved with green
    The downward ravine
Which slopes to the western gleams :

    And gliding and springing
    She went, ever singing
  In murmurs as soft as sleep.
    The Earth seemed to love her,
    And Heaven smiled above her,
  As she lingered towards the deep.

2.   Then Alpheus bold,
    On his glacier cold,
With his trident the mountains strook,
    And opened a chasm
    In the rocks—with the spasm
All Erymanthus shook.
    And the black south wind
    It concealed behind
The urns of the silent snow,
    And earthquake and thunder
    Did rend in sunder
The bars of the spirits below.
    The beard and the hair
    Of the River-god were
Seen through the torrent's sweep,
    As he followed the light
    Of the fleet Nymph's flight
To the brink of the Dorian deep.

3.   "Oh save me! Oh guide me!
    And bid the deep hide me!
For he grasps me now by the hair!"
    The loud Ocean heard,
    To its blue depth stirred,
And divided at her prayer;
    And under the water
    The Earth's white daughter

ARETHUSA.

   Fled like a sunny beam;
    Behind her descended
    Her billows, unblended
  With the brackish Dorian stream.
    Like a gloomy stain
    On the emerald main,
  Alpheus rushed behind—
    As an eagle pursuing
    A dove to its ruin
  Down the streams of the cloudy wind.

4.
    Under the bowers
    Where the Ocean Powers
  Sit on their pearlèd thrones;
    Through the coral woods
    Of the weltering floods;
  Over heaps of unvalued stones;
    Through the dim beams
    Which amid the streams
  Weave a network of coloured light;
    And under the caves
    Where the shadowy waves
  Are as green as the forest's night:
    Outspeeding the shark
    And the sword-fish dark—
  Under the ocean foam,
    And up through the rifts
    Of the mountain cliffs—
  They passed to their Dorian home.

5.
    And now from their fountains
    In Enna's mountains,
  Down one vale where the morning basks,

   Like friends once parted
   Grown single-hearted,
They ply their watery tasks.
   At sunrise they leap
   From their cradles steep
In the cave of the shelving hill;
   At noontide they flow
   Through the woods below,
And the meadows of asphodel;
   And at night they sleep
   In the rocking deep
Beneath the Ortygian shore—
   Like spirits that lie
   In the azure sky,
When they love but live no more.

Pisa.

HYMN OF APOLLO.

1. THE sleepless Hours who watch me as I lie,
   Curtained with star-inwoven tapestries
  From the broad moonlight of the sky,
Fanning the busy dreams from my dim eyes,
Waken me when their Mother, the grey Dawn,
Tells them that dreams and that the moon is gone.

2. Then I arise, and, climbing heaven's blue dome,
  I walk over the mountains and the waves,
Leaving my robe upon the ocean foam—
  My footsteps pave the clouds with fire; the caves
Are filled with my bright presence; and the air
Leaves the green Earth to my embraces bare.

3. The sunbeams are my shafts, with which I kill
    Deceit, that loves the night and fears the day ;
All men who do or even imagine ill
    Fly me, and from the glory of my ray
Good minds and open actions take new might,
Until diminished by the reign of Night.

4. I feed the clouds, the rainbows, and the flowers,
    With their ethereal colours ; the moon's globe,
And the pure stars in their eternal bowers,
    Are cinctured with my power as with a robe ;
Whatever lamps on earth or heaven may shine
Are portions of one power, which is mine.

5. I stand at noon upon the peak of heaven ;
    Then with unwilling steps I wander down
Into the clouds of the Atlantic even ;
    For grief that I depart they weep and frown.
What look is more delightful than the smile
With which I soothe them from the western isle ?

6. I am the eye with which the universe
    Beholds itself, and knows itself divine ;
All harmony of instrument or verse,
    All prophecy, all medicine, are mine,
All light of art or nature—to my song
Victory and praise in its own right belong.

HYMN OF PAN.

FROM the forests and highlands
    We come, we come;
From the river-girt islands,
    Where loud waves are dumb
Listening to my sweet pipings.
    The wind in the reeds and the rushes,
        The bees on the bells of thyme,
    The birds on the myrtle bushes,
        The cicale above in the lime,
    And the lizards below in the grass,
Were as silent as ever old Tmolus was,
    Listening to my sweet pipings.

Liquid Peneus was flowing,
    And all dark Tempe lay
In Pelion's shadow, outgrowing
    The light of the dying day,
Speeded by my sweet pipings.
    The Sileni, and Sylvans, and Fauns,
        And the Nymphs of the woods and waves,
    To the edge of the moist river-lawns,
        And the brink of the dewy caves,
And all that did then attend and follow,
Were silent with love—as you now, Apollo,
    With envy of my sweet pipings.

I sang of the dancing stars,
    I sang of the dædal earth,
And of heaven, and the Giant wars,
    And love, and death, and birth.
And then I changed my pipings—

Singing how down the vale of Mænalus
  I pursued a maiden, and clasped a reed :
Gods and men, we are all deluded thus ;
  It breaks in our bosom, and then we bleed.
All wept—as I think both ye now would,
If envy or age had not frozen your blood—
  At the sorrow of my sweet pipings.

THE QUESTION.

1. I DREAMED that, as I wandered by the way,
      Bare winter suddenly was changed to Spring ;
    And gentle odours led my steps astray,
      Mixed with a sound of waters murmuring
    Along a shelving bank of turf, which lay
      Under a copse, and hardly dared to fling
    Its green arms round the bosom of the stream,
    But kissed it and then fled, as thou mightest in dream.

2. There grew pied wind-flowers and violets ;
      Daisies, those pearled Arcturi of the earth,
    The constellated flower that never sets ;
      Faint oxlips ; tender bluebells, at whose birth
    The sod scarce heaved ; and that tall flower that wets—
      Like a child, half in tenderness and mirth—
    Its mother's face with heaven-collected tears
    When the low wind its playmate's voice it hears.

THE QUESTION.

3. And in the warm hedge grew lush eglantine,
      Green cow-bind and the moonlight-coloured may,
   And cherry-blossoms, and white cups whose wine
      Was the bright dew yet drained not by the Day;
   And wild roses, and ivy serpentine,
      With its dark buds and leaves wandering astray;
   And flowers, azure, black, and streaked with gold,
   Fairer than any wakened eyes behold.

4. And nearer to the river's trembling edge
      There grew broad flag-flowers, purple pranked with white,
   And starry river-buds among the sedge,
      And floating water-lilies, broad and bright,
   Which lit the oak that overhung the hedge
      With moonlight beams of their own watery light;
   And bulrushes, and reeds of such deep green
   As soothed the dazzled eye with sober sheen.

5. Methought that of these visionary flowers
      I made a nosegay, bound in such a way
   That the same hues which in their natural bowers
      Were mingled or opposed, the like array
   Kept these imprisoned children of the Hours
      Within my hand—and then, elate and gay,
   I hastened to the spot whence I had come,
   That I might there present it—oh! to whom?

THE SENSITIVE PLANT.

PART I.

1. A SENSITIVE Plant in a garden grew ;
   And the young winds fed it with silver dew ;
   And it opened its fan-like leaves to the light,
   And closed them beneath the kisses of Night.

2. And the Spring arose on the garden fair,
   Like the Spirit of Love felt everywhere ;
   And each flower and herb on earth's dark breast
   Rose from the dreams of its wintry rest.

3. But none ever trembled and panted with bliss
   In the garden, the field, or the wilderness,
   Like a doe in the noontide with love's sweet want,
   As the companionless Sensitive Plant.

4. The snowdrop, and then the violet,
   Arose from the ground with warm rain wet ;
   And their breath was mixed with fresh odour sent
   From the turf, like the voice and the instrument.

5. Then the pied wind-flowers and the tulip tall,
   And narcissi, the fairest among them all,
   Who gaze on their eyes in the stream's recess
   Till they die of their own dear loveliness ;

6. And the Naiad-like lily of the vale,
   Whom youth makes so fair, and passion so pale,
   That the light of its tremulous bells is seen
   Through their pavilions of tender green ;

7. And the hyacinth, purple, and white, and blue,
   Which flung from its bells a sweet peal anew

Of music so delicate, soft, and intense,
It was felt like an odour within the sense;

8. And the rose, like a nymph to the bath addressed,
Which unveiled the depth of her glowing breast,
Till, fold after fold, to the fainting air
The soul of her beauty and love lay bare;

9. And the wand-like lily, which lifted up,
As a Mænad, its moonlight-coloured cup,
Till the fiery star which is its eye
Gazed through clear dew on the tender sky;

10. And the jessamine faint, and the sweet tuberose—
The sweetest flower for scent that blows—
And all rare blossoms from every clime,
Grew in that garden in purest prime.

11. And on the stream whose inconstant bosom
Was pranked under boughs of embowering blossom,
With golden and green light slanting through
Their heaven of many a tangled hue,

12. Broad water-lilies lay tremulously,
And starry river-buds glimmered by;
And around them the soft stream did glide and dance
With a motion of sweet sound and radiance.

13. And the sinuous paths of lawn and of moss
Which led through the garden along and across,
Some open at once to the sun and the breeze,
Some lost among bowers of blossoming trees,

14. Were all paved with daisies and delicate bells
As fair as the fabulous asphodels,

And flowerets which, drooping as day drooped too,
Fell into pavilions, white, purple, and blue,
To roof the glow-worm from the evening dew.

15. And from this undefiled paradise
The flowers (as an infant's awakening eyes
Smile on its mother, whose singing sweet
Can first lull and at last must awaken it),

16. When heaven's blithe winds had unfolded them
As mine-lamps enkindle a hidden gem,
Shone smiling to heaven, and every one
Shared joy in the light of the gentle sun;

17. For each one was interpenetrated
With the light and the odour its neighbour shed,
Like young lovers whom youth and love make dear,
Wrapped and filled by their mutual atmosphere.

18. But the Sensitive Plant, which could give small fruit
Of the love which it felt from the leaf to the root,
Received more than all; it loved more than ever,
Where none wanted but it, could belong to the giver—

19. For the Sensitive Plant has no bright flower;
Radiance and odour are not its dower;
It loves even like Love—its deep heart is full;
It desires what it has not, the beautiful.

20. The light winds which from unsustaining wings
Shed the music of many murmurings;
The beams which dart from many a star
Of the flowers whose hues they bear afar;

21. The plumèd insects swift and free,
    Like golden boats on a sunny sea,
    Laden with light and odour, which pass
    Over the gleam of the living grass ;

22. The unseen clouds of the dew which lie
    Like fire in the flowers till the sun rides high,
    Then wander like spirits among the spheres,
    Each cloud faint with the fragrance it bears ;

23. The quivering vapours of dim noontide,
    Which like a sea o'er the warm earth glide,
    In which every sound, and odour, and beam
    Move as reeds in a single stream—

24. Each and all like ministering angels were
    For the Sensitive Plant sweet joy to bear,
    Whilst the lagging hours of the day went by,
    Like windless clouds o'er a tender sky.

25. And, when evening descended from heaven above,
    And the earth was all rest, and the air was all love,
    And delight, though less bright, was far more deep,
    And the day's veil fell from the world of sleep—

26. And the beasts, and the birds, and the insects were drowned
    In an ocean of dreams without a sound,
    Whose waves never mark though they ever impress
    The light sand which paves it, consciousness—

27. (Only overhead the sweet nightingale
    Ever sang more sweet as the day might fail,
    And snatches of its elysian chant
    Were mixed with the dream of the Sensitive Plant)—

28. The Sensitive Plant was the earliest
    Upgathered into the bosom of rest;
    A sweet child weary of its delight,
    The feeblest and yet the favourite,
    Cradled within the embrace of Night.

PART II.

1. THERE was a power in this sweet place,
   An Eve in this Eden; a ruling Grace
   Which to the flowers, did they waken or dream,
   Was as God is to the starry scheme.

2. A Lady, the wonder of her kind,
   Whose form was upborne by a lovely mind,
   Which, dilating, had moulded her mien and motion
   Like a sea-flower unfolded beneath the ocean,

3. Tended the garden from morn to even:
   And the meteors of that sublunar heaven,
   Like the lamps of the air when Night walks forth,
   Laughed round her footsteps up from the earth.

4. She had no companion of mortal race;
   But her tremulous breath and her flushing face
   Told, whilst the morn kissed the sleep from her eyes,
   That her dreams were less slumber than paradise:

5. As if some bright Spirit for her sweet sake
   Had deserted heaven while the stars were awake,
   As if yet around her he lingering were,
   Though the veil of daylight concealed him from her.

6. Her step seemed to pity the grass it pressed:
   You might hear, by the heaving of her breast,

That the coming and going of the wind
Brought pleasure there, and left passion behind.

7. And, wherever her airy footstep trod,
Her trailing hair from the grassy sod
Erased its light vestige with shadowy sweep,
Like a sunny storm o'er the dark-green deep.

8. I doubt not the flowers of that garden sweet
Rejoiced in the sound of her gentle feet;
I doubt not they felt the spirit that came
From her glowing fingers through all their frame.

9. She sprinkled bright water from the stream
On those that were faint with the sunny beam;
And out of the cups of the heavy flowers
She emptied the rain of the thunder-showers.

10. She lifted their heads with her tender hands,
And sustained them with rods and osier bands;
If the flowers had been her own infants, she
Could never have nursed them more tenderly.

11. And all killing insects and gnawing worms,
And things of obscene and unlovely forms,
She bore in a basket of Indian woof
Into the rough woods far aloof—

12. In a basket of grasses and wild flowers full,
The freshest her gentle hands could pull
For the poor banished insects, whose intent,
Although they did ill, was innocent.

13. But the bee, and the beamlike ephemeris   [kiss
Whose path is the lightning's, and soft moths that

The sweet lips of the flowers, and harm not, did she
Make her attendant angels be.

14. And many an antenatal tomb
Where butterflies dream of the life to come
She left clinging round the smooth and dark
Edge of the odorous cedar bark.

15. This fairest Creature from earliest Spring
Thus moved through the garden ministering
All the sweet season of summer tide:
And, ere the first leaf looked brown, she died.

PART III.

1. THREE days the flowers of the garden fair
Like stars when the moon is awakened were,
Or the waves of Baiæ ere luminous
She floats up through the smoke of Vesuvius.

2. And on the fourth the Sensitive Plant
Felt the sound of the funeral chant;
And the steps of the bearers, heavy and slow;
And the sobs of the mourners, deep and low;

3. The weary sound and the heavy breath;
And the silent motions of passing death;
And the smell, cold, oppressive, and dank,
Sent through the pores of the coffin plank.

4. The dark grass, and the flowers among the grass,
Were bright with tears as the crowd did pass;
From their sighs the Wind caught a mournful tone,
And sate in the pines, and gave groan for groan.

5. The garden, once fair, became cold and foul,
   Like the corpse of her who had been its soul;
   Which at first was lovely as if in sleep,
   Then slowly changed, till it grew a heap
   To make men tremble who never weep.

6. Swift summer into the autumn flowed;
   And frost in the mist of the morning rode,
   Though the noonday sun looked clear and bright,
   Mocking the spoil of the secret night.

7. The rose-leaves, like flakes of crimson snow,
   Paved the turf and the moss below:
   The lilies were drooping, and white, and wan,
   Like the head and the skin of a dying man;

8. And Indian plants, of scent and hue
   The sweetest that ever were fed on dew,
   Leaf after leaf, day after day,
   Were massed into the common clay.

9. And the leaves, brown, yellow, and grey, and red,
   And white with the whiteness of what is dead,
   Like troops of ghosts on the dry wind passed:
   Their whistling noise made the birds aghast.

10. And the gusty winds waked the wingèd seeds
    Out of their birthplace of ugly weeds,
    Till they clung round many a sweet flower's stem,
    Which rotted into the earth with them.

11. The water-blooms under the rivulet
    Fell from the stalks on which they were set;
    And the eddies drove them here and there,
    As the winds did those of the upper air.

THE SENSITIVE PLANT.

12. Then the rain came down ; and the broken stalks
    Were bent and tangled across the walks ;
    And the leafless network of parasite bowers
    Massed into ruin, and all sweet flowers.

13. Between the time of the wind and the snow,
    All loathliest weeds began to grow,
    Whose coarse leaves were splashed with many a speck,
    Like the water-snake's belly and the toad's back ;

14. And thistles, and nettles, and darnels rank,
    And the dock, and henbane ; and hemlock dank
    Stretched out its long and hollow shank,
    And stifled the air till the dead wind stank.

15. And plants at whose names the verse feels loth
    Filled the place with a monstrous undergrowth,
    Prickly, and pulpous, and blistering, and blue,
    Livid, and starred with a lurid dew.

16. And agarics and fungi, with mildew and mould,
    Started like mist from the wet ground cold ;
    Pale, fleshy, as if the decaying dead
    With a spirit of growth had been animated.

17. Their moss rotted off them flake by flake,
    Till the thick stalk stuck like a murderer's stake,
    Where rags of loose flesh yet tremble on high,
    Infecting the winds that wander by.

18. Spawn, weeds, and filth, a leprous scum,
    Made the running rivulet thick and dumb,
    And at its outlet flags huge as stakes
    Dammed it up with roots knotted like water-snakes.

19. And hour by hour, when the air was still,
    The vapours arose which have strength to kill:
    At morn they were seen, at noon they were felt,
    At night they were darkness no star could melt.

20. And unctuous meteors from spray to spray
    Crept and flitted in broad noonday
    Unseen; every branch on which they alit
    By a venomous blight was burned and bit.

21. The Sensitive Plant, like one forbid,
    Wept, and the tears within each lid
    Of its folded leaves which together grew,
    Were changed to a blight of frozen glue.

22. For the leaves soon fell, and the branches soon
    By the heavy axe of the blast were hewn;
    The sap shrank to the root through every pore,
    As blood to a heart that will beat no more.

23. For Winter came: the wind was his whip;
    One choppy finger was on his lip:
    He had torn the cataracts from the hills,
    And they clanked at his girdle like manacles.

24. His breath was a chain which without a sound
    The earth, and the air, and the water bound;
    He came, fiercely driven in his chariot-throne
    By the tenfold blasts of the Arctic zone.

25. Then the weeds, which were forms of living death,
    Fled from the frost to the earth beneath:
    Their decay and sudden flight from frost
    Was but like the vanishing of a ghost.

26. And under the roots of the Sensitive Plant
　　The moles and the dormice died for want:
　　The birds dropped stiff from the frozen air,
　　And were caught in the branches naked and bare.

27. First there came down a thawing rain,
　　And its dull drops froze on the boughs again;
　　Then there steaméd up a freezing dew
　　Which to the drops of the thaw-rain grew;

28. And a northern Whirlwind, wandering about
　　Like a wolf that had smelt a dead child out,
　　Shook the boughs, thus laden, and heavy, and stiff,
　　And snapped them off with his rigid griff.

29. When Winter had gone, and Spring came back,
　　The Sensitive Plant was a leafless wreck;
　　But the mandrakes, and toadstools, and docks, and darnels
　　Rose like the dead from their ruined charnels.

CONCLUSION.

1. WHETHER the Sensitive Plant, or that
　Which within its boughs like a spirit sat
　Ere its outward form had known decay,
　Now felt this change, I cannot say.

2. Whether that Lady's gentle mind,
　No longer with the form combined
　Which scattered love as stars do light,
　Found sadness where it left delight,

3. I dare not guess. But, in this life
　Of error, ignorance, and strife,

Where nothing is but all things seem,
And we the shadows of the dream,

4. It is a modest creed, and yet
Pleasant if one considers it,
To own that death itself must be,
Like all the rest, a mockery.

5. That garden sweet, that Lady fair,
And all sweet shapes and odours there,
In truth have never passed away:
'Tis we, 'tis ours, are changed; not they.

6. For love, and beauty, and delight,
There is no death nor change; their might
Exceeds our organs, which endure
No light, being themselves obscure.

THE CLOUD.

1. I BRING fresh showers for the thirsting flowers
   From the seas and the streams;
I bear light shade for the leaves when laid
   In their noonday dreams.
From my wings are shaken the dews that waken
   The sweet buds every one,
When rocked to rest on their Mother's breast,
   As she dances about the sun.
I wield the flail of the lashing hail,
   And whiten the green plains under;
And then again I dissolve it in rain,
   And laugh as I pass in thunder.

2. I sift the snow on the mountains below,
   And their great pines groan aghast;
And all the night 'tis my pillow white,
   While I sleep in the arms of the Blast.
Sublime on the towers of my skiey bowers
   Lightning my pilot sits;
In a cavern under is fettered the Thunder,
   It struggles and howls at fits.
Over earth and ocean with gentle motion
   This pilot is guiding me,
Lured by the Love of the Genii that move
   In the depths of the purple sea;
Over the rills, and the crags, and the hills,
   Over the lakes and the plains,
Wherever he dream under mountain or stream
   The Spirit he loves remains;
And I all the while bask in heaven's blue smile,
   Whilst he is dissolving in rains.

3. The sanguine Sunrise, with his meteor eyes,
   And his burning plumes outspread,
Leaps on the back of my sailing rack,
   When the morning star shines dead:
As on the jag of a mountain crag
   Which an earthquake rocks and swings
An eagle alit one moment may sit
   In the light of its golden wings.
And, when Sunset may breathe, from the lit sea beneath
   Its ardours of rest and of love,
And the crimson pall of eve may fall
   From the depth of heaven above,
With wings folded I rest on mine airy nest,
   As still as a brooding dove.

4. That orbèd maiden with white fire laden
   Whom mortals call the Moon
Glides glimmering o'er my fleece-like floor
   By the midnight breezes strewn ;
And wherever the beat of her unseen feet,
   Which only the angels hear,
May have broken the woof of my tent's thin roof,
   The Stars peep behind her and peer.
And I laugh to see them whirl and flee
   Like a swarm of golden bees,
When I widen the rent in my wind-built tent—
   Till the calm rivers, lakes, and seas,
Like strips of the sky fallen through me on high,
   Are each paved with the moon and these.

5. I bind the Sun's throne with a burning zone,
   And the Moon's with a girdle of pearl ;
The volcanoes are dim, and the Stars reel and swim,
   When the Whirlwinds my banner unfurl.
From cape to cape, with a bridge-like shape,
   Over a torrent sea,
Sunbeam-proof, I hang like a roof ;
   The mountains its columns be.
The trumphal arch through which I march,
   With hurricane, fire, and snow,
When the Power of the air are chained to my chair
   Is the million-coloured bow ;
The Sphere-fire above its soft colours wove,
   While the moist Earth was laughing below.

6. I am the daughter of Earth and Water,
   And the nursling of the Sky :
I pass through the pores of the ocean and shores ;
   I change, but I cannot die.

For after the rain, when with never a stain
    The pavilion of heaven is bare,
And the winds, and sunbeams, with their convex
      gleams,
    Build up the blue dome of air,
I silently laugh at my own cenotaph—
    And out of the caverns of rain,
Like a child from the womb, like a ghost from the
      tomb,
    I arise, and unbuild it again.

TO A SKYLARK.

1.   HAIL to thee, blithe spirit—
      Bird thou never wert—
   That from heaven or near it
     Pourest thy full heart
In profuse strains of unpremeditated art.

2.   Higher still and higher
     From the earth thou springest:
   Like a cloud of fire,
     The blue deep thou wingest,
And singing still dost soar, and soaring ever singest.

3.   In the golden lightning
     Of the sunken sun,
   O'er which clouds are brightening,
     Thou dost float and run,
Like an embodied joy whose race is just begun.

4. The pale purple even
    Melts around thy flight;
  Like a star of heaven
    In the broad daylight,
Thou art unseen, but yet I hear thy shrill delight—

5. Keen as are the arrows
    Of that silver sphere
  Whose intense lamp narrows
    In the white dawn clear,
Until we hardly see, we feel, that it is there.

6. All the earth and air
    With thy voice is loud,
  As, when night is bare,
    From one lonely cloud
The moon rains out her beams, and heaven is overflowed.

7. What thou art we know not;
    What is most like thee?
  From the rainbow clouds there flow not
    Drops so bright to see
As from thy presence showers a rain of melody—

8. Like a poet hidden
    In the light of thought,
  Singing hymns unbidden,
    Till the world is wrought
To sympathy with hopes and fears it heeded not:

9. Like a high-born maiden
    In a palace tower,
  Soothing her love-laden
    Soul in secret hour
With music sweet as love which overflows her bower:

10. Like a glow-worm golden
    In a dell of dew,
Scattering unbeholden
    Its aërial hue
Among the flowers and grass which screen it from the view:

11. Like a rose embowered
    In its own green leaves,
By warm winds deflowered,
    Till the scent it gives
Makes faint with too much sweet these heavy wingèd thieves.

12. Sound of vernal showers
    On the twinkling grass,
Rain-awakened flowers—
    All that ever was,
Joyous, and clear, and fresh—thy music doth surpass.

13. Teach us, sprite or bird,
    What sweet thoughts are thine:
I have never heard
    Praise of love or wine
That panted forth a flood of rapture so divine.

14. Chorus hymeneal
    Or triumphal chant,
Matched with thine, would be all
    But an empty vaunt—
A thing wherein we feel there is some hidden want.

15. What objects are the fountains
    Of thy happy strain ?

What fields, or waves, or mountains ?
What shapes of sky or plain ?
What love of thine own kind ! what ignorance of pain !

16. With thy clear keen joyance
Langour cannot be :
Shadow of annoyance
Never came near thee :
Thou lovest, but ne'er knew love's sad satiety.

17. Waking or asleep,
Thou of death must deem
Things more true and deep
Than we mortals dream,
Or how could thy notes flow in such a crystal stream ?

18. We look before and after,
And pine for what is not :
Our sincerest laughter
With some pain is fraught ;
Our sweetest songs are those that tell of saddest thought.

19. Yet, if we could scorn
Hate, and pride, and fear,
If we were things born
Not to shed a tear,
I know not how thy joy we ever should come near.

20. Better than all measures
Of delightful sound,
Better than all treasures
That in books are found,
Thy skill to poet were, thou scorner of the ground !

21. Teach me half the gladness
    That thy brain must know;
Such harmonious madness
    From my lips would flow
The world should listen then as I am listening now.

TO ——

I FEAR thy kisses, gentle maiden;
    Thou needest not fear mine—
My spirit is too deeply laden
    Ever to burthen thine.

I fear thy mien, thy tones, thy motion;
    Thou needest not fear mine—
Innocent is the heart's devotion
    With which I worship thine.

THE TWO SPIRITS.

AN ALLEGORY.

FIRST SPIRIT.

O THOU who plumed with strong desire
    Wouldst float above the earth, beware!
A shadow tracks thy flight of fire—
    Night is coming!

Bright are the regions of the air,
And among the winds and beams
It were delight to wander there—
    Night is coming!

SECOND SPIRIT.

The deathless stars are bright above :
  If I would cross the shade of night,
Within my heart is the lamp of love,
    And that is day ;
And the moon will shine with gentle light
On my golden plumes where'er they move ;
  The meteors will linger round my flight,
    And make night day.

FIRST SPIRIT.

But if the whirlwinds of darkness waken
  Hail, and lightning, and stormy rain ?
See, the bounds of the air are shaken—
  The red swift clouds of the hurricane
Yon declining sun have overtaken,
  The clash of the hail sweeps over the plain—
    Night is coming!

SECOND SPIRIT.

I see the light, and I hear the sound.
I'll sail on the flood of the tempest dark,
With the calm within and the light around
    Which makes night day :
  And thou, when the gloom is deep and stark,
Look from thy dull earth, slumber-bound ;
  My moonlike flight thou then mayst mark
    On high, far away.

Some say there is a precipice
　Where one vast pine is frozen to ruin
O'er piles of snow and chasms of ice
　　'Mid Alpine mountains;
　And that the languid storm, pursuing
That wingèd shape, for ever flies
　Round those hoar branches, aye renewing
　　Its aëry fountains.

Some say, when nights are dry and clear,
　And the death-dews sleep on the morass,
Sweet whispers are heard by the traveller,
　　Which make night day:
And a silver shape like his early love doth pass,
Upborne by her wild and glittering hair;
　And, when he awakes on the fragrant grass,
　　He finds night day.

SONG OF PROSERPINE,

WHILST GATHERING FLOWERS ON THE PLAIN OF ENNA.

SACRED Goddess, Mother Earth,
　Thou from whose immortal bosom
Gods, and men, and beasts have birth,
　Leaf, and blade, and bud, and blossom,
Breathe thine influence most divine
On thine own child, Proserpine.

If with mists of evening dew
　Thou dost nourish these young flowers

Till they grow in scent and hue
Fairest children of the Hours,
Breathe thine influence most divine
On thine own child, Proserpine.

LETTER TO MARIA GISBORNE.

LEGHORN, 1st July 1820.

THE spider spreads her webs, whether she be
  In poet's tower, cellar, or barn, or tree;
The silk-worm in the dark-green mulberry leaves
His winding-sheet and cradle ever weaves:
So I, a thing whom moralists call worm,
Sit spinning still round this decaying form,
From the fine threads of rare and subtle thought—
No net of words in garish colours wrought
To catch the idle buzzers of the day—
But a soft cell where, when that fades away,
Memory may clothe in wings my living name,
And feed it with the asphodels of fame
Which in those hearts which must remember me
Grow, making love an immortality.

Whoever should behold me now, I wist,
Would think I were a mighty mechanist,
Bent with sublime Archimedean art
To breathe a soul into the iron heart
Of some machine portentous, or strange gin,
Which by the force of figured spells might win
Its way over the sea, and sport therein—

For round the walls are hung dread engines, such
As Vulcan never wrought for Jove to clutch
Ixion or the Titan ; or the quick
Wit of that man of God, Saint Dominic,
To convince atheist, Turk, or heretic ;
Or those in philanthropic councils met
Who thought to pay some interest for the debt
They owed to Jesus Christ for their salvation
By giving a faint foretaste of damnation
To Shakespeare, Sydney, Spenser, and the rest
Who made our land an island of the blessed
(When lamp-like Spain, who now relumes her fire
On Freedom's hearth, grew dim with empire),
With thumbscrews, wheels with tooth and spike and
    jag,
Which fishers found under the utmost crag
Of Cornwall, and the storm-encompassed isles
Where to the sky the rude sea seldom smiles
Unless in treacherous wrath, as on the morn
When the exulting elements in scorn,
Satiated with destroyed destruction, lay
Sleeping in beauty on their mangled prey,
As panthers sleep. And other strange and dread
Magical forms the brick floor overspread.
Proteus transformed to metal did not make
More figures, or more strange ; nor did he take
Such shapes of unintelligible brass,
Or heap himself in such a horrid mass
Of tin and iron not to be understood,
And forms of unimaginable wood,
To puzzle Tubal Cain and all his brood :
Great screws, and cones, and wheels, and groovèd
    blocks,
The elements of what will stand the shocks

Of wave and wind and time.—Upon the table
More knacks and quips there be than I am able
To catalogise in this verse of mine:
A pretty bowl of wood—not full of wine,
But quicksilver; that dew which the gnomes drink
When at their subterranean toil they swink,
Pledging the demons of the earthquake, who
Reply to them in lava—cry " Halloo ! "—
And call out to the cities o'er their head.
Roofs, towns, and shrines, the dying and the dead,
Crash through the chinks of earth; and then all quaff
Another rouse, and hold their sides and laugh.
This quicksilver no gnome has drunk ; within
The walnut bowl it lies, veinèd and thin,
In colour like the wake of light that stains
The Tuscan deep when from the moist moon rains
The inmost shower of its white fire—the breeze
Is still—blue heaven smiles over the pale seas.
And in this bowl of quicksilver—for I
Yield to the impulse of an infancy
Outlasting manhood—I have made to float
A rude idealism of a paper boat,
A hollow screw with cogs: Henry will know
The thing I mean, and laugh at me. If so
He fears not I should do more mischief.—Next
Lie bills and calculations much perplexed
With steam-boats, frigates, and machinery quaint,
Traced over them in blue and yellow paint.
Then comes a range of mathematical
Instruments, for plans nautical and statical ;
A heap of rosin ; a queer broken glass
With ink in it ; a china cup that was
(What it will never be again, I think)

A thing from which sweet lips were wont to drink
The liquor doctors rail at—and which I
Will quaff in spite of them; and, when we die,
We'll toss up who died first of drinking tea,
And cry out "Heads or tails!" where'er we be.
Near that, a dusty paint-box, some old hooks,
A half-burnt match, an ivory block, three books,
Where conic sections, spherics, logarithms,
To great Laplace from Saunderson and Sims,
Lie heaped in their harmonious disarray
Of figures—disentangle them who may.
Baron de Tott's Memoirs beside them lie,
And some odd volumes of old chemistry.
Near them a most inexplicable thing,
With lead in the middle—I'm conjecturing
How to make Henry understand; but no!
I'll leave, as Spenser says "with many mo,"
This secret in the pregnant womb of Time,
Too vast a matter for so weak a rhyme.

And here like some weird archimage sit I,
Plotting dark spells and devilish enginery—
The self-impelling steam-wheels of the mind,
Which pump up oaths from clergymen, and grind
The gentle spirit of our meek Reviews
Into a powdery foam of salt abuse,
Ruffling the ocean of their self-content.
I sit, and smile—or sigh, as is my bent,
But not for them. Libeccio rushes round
With an inconstant and an idle sound;
I heed him more than them. The thunder-smoke
Is gathering on the mountains, like a cloak
Folded athwart their shoulders broad and bare;
The ripe corn under the undulating air

Undulates like an ocean ; and the vines
Are trembling wide in all their trellised lines ;
The murmur of the awakening sea doth fill
The empty pauses of the blast ; the hill
Looks hoary through the white electric rain ;
And from the glens beyond, in sullen strain,
The interrupted thunder howls ; above
One chasm of heaven smiles, like the eye of Love
On the unquiet world ; while such things are,
How could one worth your friendship heed the war
Of worms—the shriek of the world's carrion jays,
Their censure or their wonder or their praise ?

You are not here ! The quaint witch Memory sees
In vacant chairs your absent images,
And points where once you sat, and now should be,
But are not.—I demand if ever we
Shall meet as then we met—and she replies,
Veiling in awe her second-sighted eyes,
"I know the past alone : but summon home
My sister Hope—she speaks of all to come."
But I, an old diviner who knew well
Every false verse of that sweet oracle,
Turned to the sad enchantress once again,
And sought a respite from my gentle pain
In citing every passage o'er and o'er
Of our communion—How on the sea shore
We watched the ocean and the sky together,
Under the roof of blue Italian weather :
How I ran home through last year's thunder-storm,
And felt the transverse lightning linger warm
Upon my cheek ; and how we often made
Treats for each other where good-will outweighed
The frugal luxury of our country cheer

(As it well might, were it *less* firm and clear
Than ours must ever be). And how we spun
A shroud of talk to hide us from the sun
Of this familiar life, which seems to be
But is not—or is but quaint mockery
Of all we would believe ; or sadly blame
The jarring and inexplicable frame
Of this wrong world, and then anatomise
The purposes and thoughts of men whose eyes
Were closed in distant years ; or widely guess
The issue of the earth's great business,
When we shall be as we no longer are
(Like babbling gossips safe, who hear the war
Of winds, and sigh, but tremble not) ; or how
You listened to some interrupted flow
Of visionary rhyme, in joy and pain
Struck from the inmost fountains of my brain,
With little skill perhaps ; or how we sought
Those deepest wells of passion or of thought
Wrought by wise poets in the waste of years,
Staining the sacred waters with our tears,
Quenching a thirst ever to be renewed ;
Or how I, wisest lady ! then indued
The language of a land which now is free,
And, winged with thoughts of truth and majesty,
Flits round the tyrant's sceptre like a cloud,
And bursts the peopled prisons, and cries aloud,
" My name is Legion !"—that majestic tongue
Which Calderon over the desert flung
Of ages and of nations, and which found
An echo in our hearts, and with the sound
Startled Oblivion. Thou wert then to me
As is a nurse when inarticulately
A child would talk as its grown parents do.

If living winds the rapid clouds pursue,
If hawks chase doves through the aërial way,
Huntsmen the innocent deer, and beasts their prey,
Why should not we rouse with the spirit's blast
Out of the forest of the pathless past
These recollected pleasures ?
       You are now
In London ; that great sea whose ebb and flow
At once is deaf and loud, and on the shore
Vomits its wrecks, and still howls on for more.
Yet in its depth what treasures ! You will see
That which was Godwin—greater none than he ;
Though fallen, and fallen on evil times, to stand,
Among the spirits of our age and land,
Before the dread tribunal of To-come
The foremost, whilst rebuke cowers pale and dumb.
You will see Coleridge ; he who sits obscure
In the exceeding lustre and the pure
Intense irradiation of a mind
Which, with its own internal lightning blind,
Flags wearily through darkness and despair—
A cloud-encircled meteor of the air,
A hooded eagle among blinking owls.
You will see Hunt ; one of those happy souls
Which are the salt of the earth, and without whom
This world would smell like what it is—a tomb ;
Who is what others seem. His room no doubt
Is still adorned by many a cast from Shout ;
With graceful flowers tastefully placed about,
And coronals of bay from ribbons hung,
And brighter wreaths in neat disorder flung,
The gifts of the most learned among some dozens
Of female friends, sisters-in-law, and cousins.
And there is he with his eternal puns,

Which beat the dullest brain for smiles, like duns
Thundering for money at a poet's door ;
Alas ! it is no use to say " I'm poor ! "—
Or oft in graver mood, when he will look
Things wiser than were ever read in book,
Except in Shakespeare's wisest tenderness.
You will see Hogg ; and I cannot express
His virtues (though I know that they are great),
Because he locks, then barricades, the gate
Within which they inhabit. Of his wit
And wisdom, you'll cry out when you are bit.
He is a pearl within an oyster-shell,
One of the richest of the deep. And there
Is English Peacock, with his mountain fair—
Turned into a Flamingo, that shy bird
That gleams i' the Indian air. Have you not heard,
When a man marries, dies, or turns Hindoo,
His best friends hear no more of him ? But you
Will see him, and will like him too, I hope,
With the milk-white Snowdonian antelope
Matched with this camelopard. His fine wit
Makes such a wound the knife is lost in it ;
A strain too learned for a shallow age,
Too wise for selfish bigots—let his page
Which charms the chosen spirits of the time
Fold itself up for a serener clime
Of years to come, and find its recompense
In that just expectation. Wit and sense,
Virtue and human knowledge, all that might
Make this dull world a business of delight,
Are all combined in Horace Smith. And these
(With some exceptions, which I need not teaze
Your patience by descanting on) are all
You and I know in London.

                    I recall
My thoughts, and bid you look upon the night.
As water does a sponge, so the moonlight
Fills the void, hollow, universal air.
What see you? Unpavilioned heaven is fair;
Whether the Moon, into her chamber gone,
Leaves midnight to the golden stars, or wan
Climbs with diminished beams the azure steep;
Or whether clouds sail o'er the inverse deep,
Piloted by the many-wandering blast,
And the rare stars rush through them, dim and fast.
All this is beautiful in every land.
But what see *you* beside? A shabby stand
Of hackney-coaches—a brick house or wall
Fencing some lonely court, white with the scrawl
Of our unhappy politics; or worse—
A wretched woman reeling by, whose curse,
Mixed with the watchman's, partner of her trade,
You must accept in place of serenade,
Or yellow-haired Pollonia murmuring
To Henry some unutterable thing.

I see a chaos of green leaves and fruit
Built round dark caverns, even to the root
Of the living stems who feed them, in whose bowers
There sleep in their dark dew the folded flowers.
Beyond, the surface of the unsickled corn
Trembles not in the slumbering air; and, borne
In circles quaint and ever-changing dance,
Like wingèd stars the fire-flies flash and glance,
Pale in the open moonshine, but each one
Under the dark trees seems a little sun,
A meteor tamed, a fixed star gone astray
From the silver regions of the milky way.

Afar the contadino's song is heard,
Rude but made sweet by distance, and a bird
Which cannot be a nightingale, and yet
I know none else that sings so sweet as it
At this late hour—and then all is still.
Now, Italy or London, which you will!

Next winter you must pass with me. I'll have
My house by that time turned into a grave
Of dead despondence and low-thoughted care,
And all the dreams which our tormentors are.
Oh, that Hunt, Hogg, Peacock, and Smith were there,
With everything belonging to them fair!
We will have books, Spanish, Italian, Greek;
And ask one week to make another week
As like his father as I'm unlike mine.
Though we eat little flesh and drink no wine,
Yet let's be merry. We'll have tea and toast;
Custards for supper; and an endless host
Of syllabubs and jellies and mince-pies,
And other such lady-like luxuries—
Feasting on which we will philosophise.
And we'll have fires out of the Grand Duke's wood,
To thaw the six weeks' winter in our blood.
And then we'll talk—what shall we talk about?
Oh! there are themes enough for many a bout
Of thought-entangled descant! As to nerves—
With cones, and parallelograms, and curves
I've sworn to strangle them if once they dare
To bother me, when you are with me there;
And they shall never more sip laudanum
From Helicon or Himeros. Well, come,
And in despair of * * * and of the devil
We'll make our friendly philosophic revel

Outlast the leafless time ; till buds and flowers
Warn the obscure inevitable hours
Sweet meeting by sad parting to renew—
"To-morrow to fresh woods and pastures new."

ODE TO NAPLES.

EPODE I. *a.*

I STOOD within the city disinterred ;
    And heard the autumnal leaves like light footfalls
Of spirits passing through the streets ; and heard
    The Mountain's slumberous voice at intervals
        Thrill through those roofless halls.
The oracular thunder penetrating shook
    The listening soul in my suspended blood ;
I felt that Earth out of her deep heart spoke—
    I felt, but heard not. Through white columns glowed
        The isle-sustaining ocean-flood,
A plane of light between two heavens of azure.
Around me gleamed many a bright sepulchre,
Of whose pure beauty Time, as if his pleasure
Were to spare Death, had never made erasure ;
    But every living lineament was clear
        As in the sculptor's thought, and there
The wreaths of stony myrtle, ivy, and pine,
      Like winter leaves o'ergrown by moulded snow,
        Seemed only not to move and grow
    Because the crystal silence of the air
Weighed on their life, even as the Power divine
Which then lulled all things brooded upon mine.

ODE TO NAPLES.

EPODE II. a.

Then gentle winds arose,
With many a mingled close
Of wild Æolian sound and mountain odour keen.
And where the Baian ocean
Welters, with air-like motion,
Within, above, around its bowers of starry green,
Moving the sea-flowers in those purple caves,
Even as the ever stormless atmosphere
Floats o'er the elysian realm,
It bore me (like an angel, o'er the waves
Of sunlight, whose swift pinnace of dewy air
No storm can overwhelm).
I sailed where ever flows
Under the calm serene
A spirit of deep emotion
From the unknown graves
Of the dead kings of melody.
Shadowy Aornos darkened o'er the helm
The horizontal ether; heaven stripped bare
Its depths over Elysium, where the prow
Made the invisible water white as snow;
From that Typhæan mount, Inarime,
There streamed a sunlit vapour, like the standard
Of some ethereal host;
Whilst from all the coast,   [wandered
Louder and louder, gathering round, there
Over the oracular woods and divine sea
Prophesyings which grew articulate—
They seize me—I must speak them—be they fate!

STROPHE I. a.

Naples! thou heart of men which ever pantest
Naked beneath the lidless eye of heaven!

Elysian City, which to calm enchantest
    The mutinous air and sea—they round thee, even
      As Sleep round Love, are driven !
Metropolis of a ruined paradise
    Long lost, late won, and yet but half regained !
Bright altar of the bloodless sacrifice
    Which armèd Victory offers up unstained
      To Love the flower-enchained !
Thou which wert once, and then didst cease to be,
Now art, and henceforth ever shalt be, free,
If Hope, and Truth, and Justice can avail—
      Hail, hail, all hail !

STROPHE II. *b.*

    Thou youngest giant birth
    Which from the groaning earth
Leap'st, clothed in armour of impenetrable scale !
    Last of the intercessors
    Who 'gainst the crowned transgressors
Pleadest before God's love ! arrayed in wisdom's mail,
    Wave thy lightning lance in mirth ;
    Nor let thy high heart fail,
Though from their hundred gates the leagued oppressors
With hurried legions move !   Hail, hail, all hail !

ANTISTROPHE I. *a.*

What though Cimmerian Anarchs dare blaspheme
    Freedom and thee ?   Thy shield is as a mirror
To make their blind slaves see, and with fierce gleam
    To turn his hungry sword upon the wearer ;
    A new Actæon's error
Shall theirs have been—devoured by their own hounds !

Be thou like the imperial basilisk,
Killing thy foe with unapparent wounds!
  Gaze on Oppression, till, at that dread risk
  Aghast, she pass from the earth's disk;
Fear not, but gaze—for freemen mightier grow,
And slaves more feeble, gazing on their foe.
If Hope, and Truth, and Justice may avail,
    Thou shalt be great.—All hail!

ANTISTROPHE II. b.
    From Freedom's form divine,
    From Nature's inmost shrine,
Strip every impious gawd, rend error veil by veil:
    O'er Ruin desolate,
    O'er Falsehood's fallen state,
Sit thou sublime, unawed; be the Destroyer pale!
    And equal laws be thine,
    And winged words let sail,
Freighted with truth even from the throne of God!
That wealth, surviving fate, be thine.—All hail!

STROPHE III. c.
Didst thou not start to hear Spain's thrilling pæan
  From land to land re-echoed solemnly,
Till silence became music? From the Æan
    To the cold Alps, eternal Italy
      Starts to hear thine! The sea
Which paves the desert streets of Venice laughs
  In light and music; widowed Genoa wan,
By moonlight, spells ancestral epitaphs,
  Murmuring, "Where is Doria?" fair Milan,
    Within whose veins long ran
The viper's palsying venom, lifts her heel
To bruise his head. The signal and the seal

(If Hope, and Truth, and Justice can avail)
Art thou of all these hopes.—Oh hail!

STROPHE IV. *d.*
Florence, beneath the sun,
Of cities fairest one,
Blushes within her bower for freedom's expectation:
From eyes of quenchless hope
Rome tears the priestly cope,
As ruling once by power, so now by admiration—
An athlete stripped to run
From a remoter station
For the high prize lost on Philippi's shore—
As then Hope, Truth, and Justice, did avail,
So now may Fraud and Wrong! Oh hail!

EPODE I. *b.*
Hear ye the march as of the Earth-born Forms,
 Arrayed against the ever-living gods?
The crash and darkness of a thousand storms
 Bursting their inaccessible abodes
  Of crags and thunder-clouds?
See ye the banners blazoned to the day,
 Inwrought with emblems of barbaric pride?
Dissonant threats kill silence far away;
 The serene heaven which wraps our Eden wide
  With iron light is dyed.
The Anarchs of the North lead forth their legions,
 Like chaos o'er creation, uncreating;
An hundred tribes nourished on strange religions
And lawless slaveries. Down the aerial regions
  Of the white Alps, desolating,
   Famished wolves that bide no waiting,
Blotting the glowing footsteps of old glory,

Trampling our columned cities into dust,
    Their dull and savage lust
On beauty's corse to sickness satiating—
They come! The fields they tread look black and hoary
With fire—from their red feet the streams run gory!

EPODE II. c.

Great Spirit, deepest love,
    Which rulest and dost move
All things which live and are within the Italian shore;
    Who spreadest heaven around it,
      Whose woods, rocks, waves, surround it;
Who sittest in thy star, o'er ocean's western floor!
Spirit of Beauty, at whose soft command
    The sunbeams and the showers distil its foison
      From the earth's bosom chill!
Oh bid those beams be each a blinding brand
    Of lightning! bid those showers be dew of poison!
      Bid the earth's plenty kill!
    Bid thy bright heaven above,
      Whilst light and darkness bound it,
    Be their tomb who planned
    To make it ours and thine!
Or with thine harmonising ardours fill
    And raise thy sons, as o'er the prone horizon
Thy lamp feeds every twilight wave with fire!
Be man's high hope and unextinct desire
The instrument to work thy will divine!
    Then clouds from sunbeams, antelopes from leopards,
      And frowns and fears from thee,
      Would not more swifty flee
Than Celtic wolves from the Ausonian shepherds.

Whatever, Spirit, from thy starry shrine
Thou yieldest or withholdest, oh let be
The City of thy worship ever free!

25th August 1820.

SUMMER AND WINTER.

IT was a bright and cheerful afternoon,
   Towards the end of the sunny month of June,
 When the north wind congregates in crowds
The floating mountains of the silvery clouds
From the horizon, and the stainless sky
Opens beyond them like eternity.
All things rejoiced beneath the sun—the weeds,
The river, and the cornfields, and the reeds,
The willow leaves that glanced in the light breeze,
And the firm foliage of the larger trees.

It was a Winter such as when birds die
In the deep forests; and the fishes lie
Stiffened in the translucent ice, which makes
Even the mud and slime of the warm lakes
A wrinkled clod as hard as brick; and when,
Among their children, comfortable men
Gather about great fires, and yet feel cold:
Alas then for the homeless beggar old!

LINES TO A REVIEWER.

ALAS! good friend, what profit can you see
In hating such a hateless thing as me?
There is no sport in hate, where all the rage
Is on one side. In vain would you assuage
Your frowns upon an unresisting smile,
In which not even contempt lurks, to beguile
Your heart by some faint sympathy of hate.
Oh! conquer what you cannot satiate :
For to your passion I am far more coy
Than ever yet was coldest maid or boy
    In winter noon. Of your antipathy
    If I am the Narcissus, you are free
    To pine into a sound with hating me.

AUTUMN.

A DIRGE.

THE warm sun is failing, the bleak wind is wailing,
    The bare boughs are sighing, the pale flowers are dying,
        And the Year
On the earth her death-bed, in a shroud of leaves dead,
        Is lying.
    Come, Months, come away,
    From November to May,
    In your saddest array ;
    Follow the bier
    Of the dead cold Year,
And like dim shadows watch by her sepulchre.

The chill rain is falling, the nipped worm is crawling,
The rivers are swelling, the thunder is knelling
    For the Year ;
The blithe swallows are flown, and the lizards each gone
    To his dwelling.
    Come, Months, come away ;
    Put on white, black, and grey ;
    Let your light sisters play—
    Ye, follow the bier
    Of the dead cold Year,
And make her grave green with tear on tear.

LIBERTY.

1. THE fiery mountains answer each other,
    Their thunderings are echoed from zone to zone ;
The tempestuous oceans awake one another,
    And the ice-rocks are shaken round Winter's throne,
When the clarion of the Typhoon is blown.

2. From a single cloud the lightning flashes,
    Whilst a thousand isles are illumined around ;
Earthquake is trampling one city to ashes,   [sound
    An hundred are shuddering and tottering—the
Is bellowing underground.

3. But keener thy gaze than the lightning's glare,
    And swifter thy step than the earthquake's tramp ;

Thou deafenest the rage of the ocean ; thy stare
    Makes blind the volcanoes ; the sun's bright
        lamp
    To thine is a fen-fire damp.

4. From billow, and mountain, and exhalation
    The sunlight is darted through vapour and
        blast ;
From spirit to spirit, from nation to nation,
    From city to hamlet, *thy* dawning is cast—
    And tyrants and slaves are like shadows of night
        In the van of the morning light.

THE TOWER OF FAMINE.

AMID the desolation of a city
    Which was the cradle and is now the grave
Of an extinguished people, so that Pity
    Weeps o'er the shipwrecks of oblivion's wave,
There stands the Tower of Famine. It is built
    Upon some prison-homes, whose dwellers rave
For bread, and gold, and blood : Pain linked to Guilt
    Agitates the light flame of their hours,
Until its vital oil is spent or spilt.
    There stands the pile, a tower amid the towers
And sacred domes, each marble-ribbèd roof,
    The brazen-gated temples, and the bowers
Of solitary wealth. The tempest-proof
    Pavilions of the dark Italian air
Are by its presence dimmed—they stand aloof,
    And are withdrawn—so that the world is bare—

As if a spectre, wrapped in shapeless terror,
  Amid a company of ladies fair
Should glide and glow, till it became a mirror
  Of all their beauty—and their hair and hue,
The life of their sweet eyes with all its error,
  Should be absorbed till they to marble grew.

GOOD-NIGHT.

"GOOD-NIGHT!" No, love! the night is ill
    Which severs those it should unite;
Let us remain together still—
    Then it will be *good* night.

How were the night without thee good,
    Though thy sweet wishes wing its flight?
Be it not said, thought, understood—
    Then it will be *good* night.

The hearts that on each other beat
    From evening close to morning light
Have nights as good as they are sweet,
    But never *say* "good-night."

TIME LONG PAST.

LIKE the ghost of a dear friend dead
        Is time long past.
A tone which is now forever fled,
A hope which is now forever past,

A love so sweet it could not last,
           Was time long past.

There were sweet dreams in the night
           Of time long past:
And, was it sadness or delight,
Each day a shadow onward cast
Which made us wish it yet might last—
           That time long past.

There is regret, almost remorse,
           For time long past.
'Tis like a child's belovèd corse
A father watches, till at last
Beauty is like remembrance cast
           From time long past.

SONNET.

YE hasten to the dead: what seek ye there,
   Ye restless thoughts and busy purposes
Of the idle brain, which the world's livery wear ;
  O thou quick heart, which pantest to possess
All that anticipation feigneth fair—
  Thou vainly curious mind which wouldest guess
Whence thou didst come and whither thou mayst go,
And that which never yet was known wouldst know—
  Oh! whither hasten ye, that thus ye press
With such swift feet life's green and pleasant path,
Seeking alike from happiness and woe
  A refuge in the cavern of grey death ?   [thou
O heart, and mind, and thoughts! what thing dost
Hope to inherit in the grave below ?

ADONAIS;

AN ELEGY ON THE DEATH OF JOHN KEATS

1. I WEEP for Adonais—he is dead!
    Oh! weep for Adonais, though our tears
   Thaw not the frost which binds so dear a head!
     And thou, sad Hour selected from all years
     To mourn our loss, rouse thy obscure compeers,
   And teach them thine own sorrow! Say: "With me
     Died Adonais! Till the future dares
   Forget the past, his fate and fame shall be
   An echo and a light unto eternity."

2. Where wert thou, mighty Mother, when he lay,
     When thy son lay, pierced by the shaft which flies
   In darkness? Where was lorn Urania
     When Adonais died? With veiled eyes,
     'Mid listening Echoes, in her paradise
   She sate, while one, with soft enamoured breath,
     Rekindled all the fading melodies
   With which, like flowers that mock the corse beneath,
   He had adorned and hid the coming bulk of Death.

3. Oh! weep for Adonais—he is dead!
   Wake, melancholy Mother, wake and weep!—
 Yet wherefore? Quench within their burning bed
   Thy fiery tears, and let thy loud heart keep,
   Like his, a mute and uncomplaining sleep;
 For he is gone where all things wise and fair
   Descend. Oh! dream not that the amorous deep
 Will yet restore him to the vital air; [despair.
 Death feeds on his mute voice, and laughs at our

4. Most musical of mourners, weep again!
   Lament anew, Urania!—He died
 Who was the sire of an immortal strain,
   Blind, old, and lonely, when his country's pride
   The priest, the slave, and the liberticide,
 Trampled and mocked with many a loathèd rite
   Of lust and blood. He went unterrified
 Into the gulf of death; but his clear sprite
 Yet reigns o'er earth, the third among the Sons of
   Light.

5. Most musical of mourners, weep anew!
   Not all to that bright station dared to climb;
 And happier they their happiness who knew,
   Whose tapers yet burn through that night of time
   In which suns perished. Others more sublime,
 Struck by the envious wrath of man or god,
   Have sunk, extinct in their refulgent prime;
 And some yet live, treading the thorny road
 Which leads, through toil and hate, to Fame's serene
   abode.

6. But now thy youngest, dearest one has perished,
   The nursling of thy widowhood, who grew,

　　　　Like a pale flower by some sad maiden cherished.
　　　　And fed with true-love tears instead of dew.
　　　　Most musical of mourners, weep anew!
　　　　Thy extreme hope, the loveliest and the last,
　　　　　The bloom whose petals, nipped before they blew
　　　　Died on the promise of the fruit, is waste;
　　The broken lily lies—the storm is overpassed.

7.　　To that high Capital where kingly Death
　　　　　Keeps his pale court in beauty and decay
　　　　He came; and bought, with price of purest breath,
　　　　　A grave among the eternal.—Come away!
　　　　Haste, while the vault of blue Italian day
　　　　Is yet his fitting charnel-roof, while still
　　　　　He lies as if in dewy sleep he lay.
　　　　Awake him not! surely he takes his fill
　　Of deep and liquid rest, forgetful of all ill.

8.　　He will awake no more, oh never more!
　　　　　Within the twilight chamber spreads apace
　　　　The shadow of white Death, and at the door
　　　　　Invisible Corruption waits to trace
　　　　His extreme way to her dim dwelling-place;
　　　　The Eternal Hunger sits, but pity and awe
　　　　　Soothe her pale rage, nor dares she to deface
　　　　So fair a prey, till darkness and the law
　　Of change shall o'er his sleep the mortal curtain draw

9.　　Oh weep for Adonais!—The quick Dreams,
　　　　　The passion-wingèd ministers of thought,
　　　　Who were his flocks, whom near the living streams
　　　　　Of his young spirit he fed, and whom he taught
　　　　The love which was its music, wander not—

Wander no more from kindling brain to brain,
  But droop there whence they sprung; and mourn their lot
Round the cold heart where, after their sweet pain,
They ne'er will gather strength or find a home again.

10. And one with trembling hand clasps his cold head,
      And fans him with her moonlight wings, and cries,
    "Our love, our hope, our sorrow, is not dead!
      See, on the silken fringe of his faint eyes,
      Like dew upon a sleeping flower, there lies
    A tear some Dream has loosened from his brain."
      Lost angel of a ruined paradise!
      She knew not 'twas her own—as with no stain
    She faded, like a cloud which had outwept its rain.

11. One from a lucid urn of starry dew
      Washed his light limbs, as if embalming them;
    Another clipt her profuse locks, and threw
      The wreath upon him, like an anadem
      Which frozen tears instead of pearls begem;
    Another in her wilful grief would break
      Her bow and wingèd reeds, as if to stem
    A greater loss with one which was more weak,
    And dull the barbèd fire against his frozen cheek.

12. Another Splendour on his mouth alit,
      That mouth whence it was wont to draw the breath
    Which gave it strength to pierce the guarded wit,
      And pass into the panting heart beneath
      With lightning and with music; the damp death
    Quenched its caress upon his icy lips;
      And, as a dying meteor stains a wreath

        Of moonlight vapour which the cold night clips,
  It flushed through his pale limbs, and passed to its
        eclipse.

13. And others came—Desires and Adorations,
      Wingèd Persuasions, and veiled Destinies,
  Splendours, and Glooms, and glimmering incarnations
      Of Hopes and Fears, and twilight Fantasies.
    And Sorrow, with her family of Sighs,
  And Pleasure, blind with tears, led by the gleam
      Of her own dying smile instead of eyes,
  Came in slow pomp—the moving pomp might seem
Like pageantry of mist on an autumnal stream.

14. All he had loved, and moulded into thought
      From shape, and hue, and odour, and sweet sound,
  Lamented Adonais. Morning sought
      Her eastern watch-tower, and her hair unbound,
      Wet with the tears which should adorn the ground,
  Dimmed the aërial eyes that kindle day ;
      Afar the melancholy Thunder moaned,
  Pale Ocean in unquiet slumber lay,   [dismay.
And the wild Winds flew round, sobbing in their

15. Lost Echo sits amid the voiceless mountains,
      And feeds her grief with his remembered lay,
  And will no more reply to winds or fountains,
      Or amorous birds perched on the young green spray,
      Or herdsman's horn, or bell at closing day ;
  Since she can mimic not his lips, more dear
      Than those for whose disdain she pined away
  Into a shadow of all sounds—a drear
Murmur, between their songs, is all the woodmen hear.

16. Grief made the young Spring wild, and she threw
    down
      Her kindling buds, as if she Autumn were,
    Or they dead leaves; since her delight is flown,
      For whom should she have waked the sullen
        Year?
    To Phœbus was not Hyacinth so dear,
    Nor to himself Narcissus, as to both
      Thou, Adonais; wan they stand and sere
    Amid the faint companions of their youth,
    With dew all turned to tears—odour, to sighing
      ruth.

17. Thy spirit's sister, the lorn nightingale,
      Mourns not her mate with such melodious pain;
    Not so the eagle, who like thee could scale
      Heaven, and could nourish in the sun's domain
      Her mighty youth with morning, doth complain,
    Soaring and screaming round her empty nest,
      As Albion wails for thee: the curse of Cain
    Light on his head who pierced thy innocent breast,
    And scared the angel song that was its earthly guest!

18. Ah woe is me! Winter is come and gone,
      But grief returns with the revolving year.
    The airs and streams renew their joyous tone;
      The ants, the bees, the swallows, re-appear;
      Fresh leaves and flowers deck the dead Season's
        bier;
    The amorous birds now pair in every brake,
      And build their mossy homes in field and brere;
    And the green lizard and the golden snake,
    Like unimprisoned flames, out of their trance awake.

19. Through wood, and stream, and field, and hill, and
       ocean,
           A quickening life from the Earth's heart has
               burst,
       As it has ever done, with change and motion,
           From the great morning of the world when first
           God dawned on chaos. In its steam immersed,
       The lamps of heaven flash with a softer light;
           All baser things pant with life's sacred thirst,
       Diffuse themselves, and spend in love's delight
   The beauty and the joy of their renewèd might.

20. The leprous corpse, touched by this spirit tender,
           Exhales itself in flowers of gentle breath:
       Like incarnations of the stars, when splendour
           Is changed to fragrance, they illumine death,
           And mock the merry worm that wakes beneath.
       Nought we know dies: shall that alone which knows
           Be as a sword consumed before the sheath
       By sightless lightning! The intense atom glows
   A moment, then is quenched in a most cold repose.

21. Alas that all we loved of him should be,
           But for our grief, as if it had not been,
       And grief itself be mortal! Woe is me!
           Whence are we, and why are we? of what scene
           The actors or spectators? Great and mean
       Meet massed in death, who lends what life must
               borrow.
           As long as skies are blue and fields are green,
       Evening must usher night, night urge the morrow,
   Month follow month with woe, and year wake year to
               sorrow.

22. *He* will awake no more, oh, never more!
     "Wake thou," cried Misery, "childless Mother!
       Rise
     Out of thy sleep, and slake in thy heart's core
       A wound more fierce than his, with tears and
         sighs."
     And all the Dreams that watched Urania's eyes,
     And all the Echoes whom their Sister's song
       Had held in holy silence, cried, "Arise!"
     Swift as a thought by the snake memory stung,
   From her ambrosial rest the fading Splendour sprung.

23. She rose like an autumnal Night that springs
       Out of the east, and follows wild and drear
     The golden Day, which, on eternal wings,
       Even as a ghost abandoning a bier,
       Had left the Earth a corpse. Sorrow and fear
     So struck, so roused, so rapt, Urania;
       So saddened round her like an atmosphere
     Of stormy mist; so swept her on her way,
   Even to the mournful place where Adonais lay.

24. Out of her secret paradise she sped,
       Through camps and cities rough with stone and
         steel
     And human hearts, which, to her aëry tread
       Yielding not, wounded the invisible
       Palms of her tender feet where'er they fell.
     And barbèd tongues, and thoughts more sharp than
         they,
       Rent the soft form they never could repel,
     Whose sacred blood, like the young tears of May,
   Paved with eternal flowers that undeserving way.

25. In the death-chamber for a moment Death,
    Shamed by the presence of that living might,
Blushed to annihilation, and the breath
    Revisited those lips, and life's pale light,
    Flashed through those limbs so late her dear
        delight.
"Leave me not wild, and drear, and comfortless,
    As silent lightning leaves the starless night!
Leave me not!" cried Urania. Her distress
Roused Death: Death rose and smiled, and met her
        vain caress.

26. "Stay yet awhile! speak to me once again!
    Kiss me, so long but as a kiss may live!
And in my heartless breast and burning brain
    That word, that kiss, shall all thoughts else
        survive,
    With food of saddest memory kept alive,
Now thou art dead, as if it were a part
    Of thee, my Adonais! I would give
All that I am, to be as thou now art—
But I am chained to Time, and cannot thence depart.

27. "O gentle child, beautiful as thou wert,
    Why didst thou leave the trodden paths of men
Too soon, and with weak hands though mighty
        heart
    Dare the unpastured dragon in his den?
    Defenceless as thou wert, oh! where was then
Wisdom the mirrored shield, or scorn the spear?—
    Or, hadst thou waited the full cycle when
Thy spirit should have filled its crescent sphere,
The monsters of life's waste had fled from thee like
        deer.

28. "The herded wolves bold only to pursue,
   The obscene ravens clamorous o'er the dead,
The vultures to the conqueror's banner true,
   Who feed where desolation first has fed,
   And whose wings rain contagion—how they fled,
When, like Apollo from his golden bow,
   The Pythian of the age one arrow sped,
And smiled!—The spoilers tempt no second blow,
They fawn on the proud feet that spurn them lying low.

29. "The sun comes forth, and many reptiles spawn;
   He sets, and each ephemeral insect then
Is gathered into death without a dawn,
   And the immortal stars awake again.
   So is it in the world of living men:
A godlike mind soars forth, in its delight
   Making earth bare and veiling heaven; and, when
It sinks, the swarms that dimmed or shared its light
Leave to its kindred lamps the spirit's awful night."

30. Thus ceased she: and the Mountain Shepherds came,
   Their garlands sere, their magic mantles rent.
The Pilgrim of Eternity, whose fame
   Over his living head like heaven is bent,
   An early but enduring monument,
Came, veiling all the lightnings of his song
   In sorrow. From her wilds Ierne sent
The sweetest lyrist of her saddest wrong,
And love taught grief to fall like music from his tongue.

31. 'Midst others of less note came one frail form,
   A phantom among men, companionless

As the last cloud of an expiring storm
  Whose thunder is its knell. He, as I guess,
Had gazed on Nature's naked loveliness
Actæon-like; and now he fled astray
  With feeble steps o'er the world's wilderness,
And his own thoughts along that rugged way
Pursued like raging hounds their father and their prey.

32. A pard-like Spirit beautiful and swift—
  A love in desolation masked—a power
Girt round with weakness; it can scarce uplift
  The weight of the superincumbent hour.
  It is a dying lamp, a falling shower,
A breaking billow—even whilst we speak
  Is it not broken? On the withering flower
The killing sun smiles brightly: on a cheek
The life can burn in blood even while the heart may break.

33. His head was bound with pansies overblown,
  And faded violets, white, and pied, and blue;
And a light spear topped with a cypress cone,
  Round whose rude shaft dark ivy-tresses grew
  Yet dripping with the forest's noonday dew,
Vibrated, as the ever-beating heart
  Shook the weak hand that grasped it. Of that crew
He came the last, neglected and apart;
A herd-abandoned deer struck by the hunter's dart.

34. All stood aloof, and at his partial moan
  Smiled through their tears. Well knew that gentle band
Who in another's fate now wept his own.
  As in the accents of an unknown land

He sang new sorrow, sad Urania scanned
  The Stranger's mien, and murmured, "Who art
    thou ?"
He answered not, but with a sudden hand
Made bare his branded and ensanguined brow,
  Which was like Cain's or Christ's—Oh ! that it should
    be so !

35. What softer voice is hushed over the dead ?
      Athwart what brow is that dark mantle thrown ?
    What form leans sadly o'er the white death-bed,
      In mockery of monumental stone,
      The heavy heart heaving without a moan ?
    If it be he who, gentlest of the wise,
      Taught, soothed, loved, honoured, the departed
        one,
    Let me not vex with inharmonious sighs
    The silence of that heart's accepted sacrifice.

36. Our Adonais has drunk poison—oh !
      What deaf and viperous murderer could crown
    Life's early cup with such a draught of woe ?
      The nameless worm would now itself disown ;
      It felt, yet could escape, the magic tone
    Whose prelude held all envy, hate, and wrong,
      But what was howling in one breast alone,
    Silent with expectation of the song
    Whose master's hand is cold, whose silver lyre unstrung.

37. Live thou, whose infamy is not thy fame !
      Live ! fear no heavier chastisement from me,
    Thou noteless blot on a remembered name !
      But be thyself, and know thyself to be !
      And ever at thy season be thou free

To spill the venom when thy fangs o'erflow;
  Remorse and self-contempt shall cling to thee,
Hot shame shall burn upon thy secret brow,
And like a beaten hound tremble thou shalt—as now.

38. Nor let us weep that our delight is fled
  Far from these carrion-kites that scream below.
He wakes or sleeps with the enduring dead;
  Thou canst not soar where he is sitting now.
  Dust to the dust: but the poor spirit shall flow
Back to the burning fountain whence it came,
  A portion of the Eternal, which must glow
Through time and change, unquenchably the same,
Whilst thy cold embers choke the sordid hearth of shame.

39. Peace, peace! he is not dead, he doth not sleep!
  He hath awakened from the dream of life.
'Tis we who, lost in stormy visions, keep
  With phantoms an unprofitable strife,
  And in mad trance strike with our spirit's knife
Invulnerable nothings. *We* decay
  Like corpses in a charnel; fear and grief
Convulse us and consume us day by day,
And cold hopes swarm like worms within our living clay.

40. He has outsoared the shadow of our night.
  Envy and calumny, and hate and pain
And that unrest which men miscall delight,
  Can touch him not and torture not again.
  From the contagion of the world's slow stain
He is secure; and now can never mourn
  A heart grown cold, a head grown grey, in vain—

Nor, when the spirit's self has ceased to burn,
With sparkless ashes load an unlamented urn.

41. He lives, he wakes—'tis Death is dead, not he ;
　　Mourn not for Adonais.—Thou young Dawn,
　Turn all thy dew to splendour, for from thee
　　The spirit thou lamentest is not gone !
　　Ye caverns and ye forests, cease to moan !
　Cease, ye faint flowers and fountains ! and, thou Air,
　　Which like a mourning veil thy scarf hadst thrown
　O'er the abandoned Earth, now leave it bare
Even to the joyous stars which smile on its despair !

42. He is made one with Nature. There is heard
　　His voice in all her music, from the moan
　Of thunder to the song of night's sweet bird.
　　He is a presence to be felt and known
　　In darkness and in light, from herb and stone ;
　Spreading itself where'er that Power may move
　　Which has withdrawn his being to its own,
　Which wields the world with never-wearied love,
Sustains it from beneath, and kindles it above.

43. He is a portion of the loveliness
　　Which once he made more lovely. He doth bear
　His part, while the One Spirit's plastic stress
　　Sweeps through the dull dense world ; compelling there
　　All new successions to the forms they wear ;
　Torturing the unwilling dross, that checks its flight,
　　To its own likeness, as each mass may bear ;

  And bursting in its beauty and its might
From trees, and beasts, and men, into the heaven's
   light.

44. The splendours of the firmament of time
  May be eclipsed, but are extinguished not;
Like stars to their appointed height they climb,
  And death is a low mist which cannot blot
  The brightness it may veil. When lofty thought
Lifts a young heart above its mortal lair,
  And love and life contend in it for what
Shall be its earthly doom, the dead live there,
And move like winds of light on dark and stormy
   air.

45. The inheritors of unfulfilled renown   [thought
  Rose from their thrones, built beyond mortal
Far in the unapparent. Chatterton
  Rose pale, his solemn agony had not
  Yet faded from him; Sidney, as he fought,
And as he fell, and as he lived and loved,
  Sublimely mild, a spirit without spot,
Arose: and Lucan, by his death approved;
Oblivion as they rose shrank like a thing reproved.

46. And many more, whose names on earth are dark,
  But whose transmitted effluence cannot die
So long as fire outlives the parent spark,
  Rose, robed in dazzling immortality.
  "Thou art become as one of us," they cry;
"It was for thee yon kingless sphere has long
  Swung blind in unascended majesty,
Silent alone amid an heaven of song.
Assume thy wingèd throne, thou Vesper of our throng!"

47. Who mourns for Adonais ?   Oh ! come forth,
      Fond wretch, and know thyself and him aright
   Clasp with thy panting soul the pendulous earth ;
      As from a centre, dart thy spirit's light
      Beyond all worlds, until its spacious might
   Satiate the void circumference : then shrink
      Even to a point within our day and night ;
   And keep thy heart light, lest it make thee sink,
When hope has kindled hope, and lured thee to the
      brink.

48. Or go to Rome, which is the sepulchre,
      Oh, not of him, but of our joy. 'Tis nought
   That ages, empires, and religions there
      Lie buried in the ravage they have wrought ;
      For such as he can lend—they borrow not
   Glory from those who made the world their prey ;
      And he is gathered to the kings of thought
   Who waged contention with their time's decay,
And of the past are all that cannot pass away.

49. Go thou to Rome—at once the paradise,
      The grave, the city, and the wilderness ;
   And where its wrecks like shattered mountains rise
      And flowering weeds and fragrant copses dress
      The bones of Desolation's nakedness,
   Pass, till the Spirit of the spot shall lead
      Thy footsteps to a slope of green access,
   Where, like an infant's smile, over the dead
A light of laughing flowers along the grass is spread.

50. And grey walls moulder round, on which dull Time
      Feeds, like slow fire upon a hoary brand ;

And one keen pyramid with wedge sublime,
  Pavilioning the dust of him who planned
This refuge for his memory, doth stand
Like flame transformed to marble; and beneath
  A field is spread, on which a newer band
Have pitched in heaven's smile their camp of death,
Welcoming him we lose with scarce extinguished breath.

51. Here pause. These graves are all too young as yet
  To have outgrown the sorrow which consigned
Its charge to each; and, if the seal is set
  Here on one fountain of a mourning mind,
Break it not thou! too surely shalt thou find
Thine own well full, if thou returnest home,
  Of tears and gall. From the world's bitter wind
Seek shelter in the shadow of the tomb.
What Adonais is why fear we to become!

52. The One remains, the many change and pass;
  Heaven's light for ever shines, earth's shadows fly;
Life, like a dome of many-coloured glass,
  Stains the white radiance of eternity,
  Until Death tramples it to fragments.—Die,
If thou wouldst be with that which thou dost seek!
  Follow where all is fled!—Rome's azure sky,
Flowers, ruins, statues, music—words are weak
The glory they transfuse with fitting truth to speak.

53. Why linger, why turn back, why shrink, my heart!
  Thy hopes are gone before: from all things here
They have departed; thou shouldst now depart!
  A light is past from the revolving year,

ADONAIS.

And man and woman; and what still is dear
Attracts to crush, repels to make thee wither.
The soft sky smiles, the low wind whispers near:
'Tis Adonais calls! Oh, hasten thither!
No more let life divide what death can join together.

54. That light whose smile kindles the universe,
That beauty in which all things work and move,
That benediction which the eclipsing curse
Of birth can quench not, that sustaining Love
Which, through the web of being blindly wove
By man, and beast, and earth, and air, and sea,
Burns bright or dim, as each are mirrors of
The fire for which all thirst, now beams on me,
Consuming the last clouds of cold mortality.

55. The breath whose might I have invoked in song
Descends on me; my spirit's bark is driven
Far from the shore, far from the trembling throng
Whose sails were never to the tempest given.
The massy earth and spheréd skies are riven!
I am borne darkly, fearfully, afar!
Whilst, burning through the inmost veil of heaven,
The soul of Adonais, like a star,
Beacons from the abode where the Eternal are.

POEMS WRITTEN IN 1821.

DIRGE FOR THE YEAR.

1. "ORPHAN Hours, the Year is dead!
    Come and sigh, come and weep!"
"Merry Hours, smile instead,
    For the Year is but asleep:
See, it smiles as it is sleeping,
    Mocking your untimely weeping."

2. "As an earthquake rocks a corse
    In its coffin in the clay,
So white Winter, that rough nurse,
    Rocks the dead-cold Year to-day;
Solemn Hours! wail aloud
For your Mother in her shroud."

3. "As the wild air stirs and sways
    The tree-swung cradle of a child,
So the breath of these rude Days
    Rocks the Year. Be calm and mild,
Trembling Hours; she will arise
With new love within her eyes.

4. "January grey is here,
    Like a sexton by her grave;
February bears the bier;
    March with grief doth howl and rave;
And April weeps—but O, ye Hours!
Follow with May's fairest flowers."

1st *January* 1821,

TO NIGHT.

1. SWIFTLY walk over the western wave,
            Spirit of Night!
Out of the misty eastern cave
Where, all the long and lone daylight,
Thou wovest dreams of joy and fear
Which make thee terrible and dear,
            Swift be thy flight!

2. Wrap thy form in a mantle grey,
            Star-inwrought,
Blind with thine hair the eyes of Day;
Kiss her until she be wearied out.
Then wander o'er city, and sea, and land
Touching all with thine opiate wand—
            Come, long-sought!

3. When I arose and saw the dawn,
            I sighed for thee;
When light rode high, and the dew was gone,
And noon lay heavy on flower and tree,

And the weary Day turned to her rest,
Lingering like an unloved guest,
    I sighed for thee.

4. Thy brother Death came, and cried,
    "Would'st thou me?"
Thy sweet child Sleep, the filmy-eyed,
    Murmured like a noontide bee,
"Shall I nestle near thy side?
Wouldst thou me?"—And I replied,
    "No, not thee."

5. Death will come when thou art dead,
    Soon, too soon—
Sleep will come when thou art fled.
Of neither would I ask the boon
I ask of thee, belovèd Night—
Swift be thine approaching flight,
    Come soon, soon!

FROM THE ARABIC.

AN IMITATION.

MY faint spirit was sitting in the light
    Of thy looks, my love;
It panted for thee like the hind at noon
    For the brooks, my love.
Thy barb, whose hoofs outspeed the tempest's flight,
    Bore thee far from me;
My heart, for my weak feet were weary soon,
    Did companion thee.

Ah! fleeter far than fleetest storm or steed,
    Or the death they bear,
The heart which tender thought clothes like a dove
    With the wings of care ;
In the battle, in the darkness, in the need,
    Shall mine cling to thee,
Nor claim one smile for all the comfort, love,
    It may bring to thee.

SONG.

1. RARELY, rarely comest thou,
    Spirit of Delight!
Wherefore hast thou left me now
    Many a day and night?
Many a weary night and day
'Tis since thou art fled away.

2. How shall ever one like me
    Win thee back again!
With the joyous and the free,
    Thou wilt scoff at pain.
Spirit false! thou hast forgot
All but those who need thee not.

3. As a lizard with the shade
    Of a trembling leaf,
Thou with sorrow art dismayed ;
    Even the sighs of grief
Reproach thee that thou art not near,
And reproach thou wilt not hear.

4. Let me set my mournful ditty
  To a merry measure—
Thou wilt never come for pity,
  Thou wilt come for pleasure;
Pity then will cut away
Those cruel wings, and thou wilt stay.

5. I love all that thou lovest,
  Spirit of Delight!
The fresh earth in new leaves dressed,
  And the starry night,
Autumn evening, and the morn
When the golden mists are born.

6. I love snow, and all the forms
  Of the radiant frost;
I love waves, and winds, and storms—
  Everything almost
Which is Nature's, and may be
Untainted by man's misery.

7. I love tranquil solitude,
  And such society
As is quiet, wise, and good.
  Between thee and me
What difference? But thou dost possess
The things I seek, not love them less.

8. I love Love, though he has wings,
  And like light can flee;
But above all other things,
  Spirit, I love thee—
Thou art love and life! Oh come,
Make once more my heart thy home!

TO EMILIA VIVIANI.

MADONNA, wherefore hast thou sent to me
  Sweet-basil and mignonette,
Embleming love and health, which never yet
 In the same wreath might be?
 Alas, and they are wet!
Is it with thy kisses or thy tears?
 For never rain or dew
  Such fragrance drew
From plant or flower. The very doubt endears
 My sadness ever new,
The sighs I breathe, the tears I shed, for thee.

March 1821.

LINES.

FAR, far away, O ye
  Halcyons of Memory!
Seek some far calmer nest
Than this abandoned breast;
No news of your false spring
To my heart's winter bring.
Once having gone, in vain
  Ye come again.
Vultures who build your bowers
High in the future's towers!
Withered hopes on hopes are spread:
Dying joys, choked by the dead,
 Will serve your beaks for prey
  Many a day.

TIME.

UNFATHOMABLE Sea, whose waves are years!
    Ocean of Time, whose waters of deep woe
Are brackish with the salt of human tears!
   Thou shoreless flood which in thy ebb and flow
Claspest the limits of mortality,
And, sick of prey yet howling on for more,
Vomitest thy wrecks on its inhospitable shore!
   Treacherous in calm, and terrible in storm,
     Who shall put forth on thee,
     Unfathomable Sea!

A SONG.

HE came like a dream, in the dawn of life:
    He fled like a shadow, before its noon.
He is gone, and my peace is turned to strife,
   And I wander and wane like the weary moon.
     O sweet Echo, wake,
     And for my sake
Make answer the while my heart shall break!

But my heart has a music which Echo's lips,
   Though tender and true, yet can answer not,
And the shadow that moves in the soul's eclipse
   Can return not the kiss by his now forgot;
     Sweet lips! he who hath
     On my desolate path
Cast the darkness of absence, worse than death!

ARIEL TO MIRANDA.

ARIEL to *Miranda.*—Take
This slave of Music, for the sake
Of him who is the slave of thee;
And teach it all the harmony
In which thou canst, and only thou,
Make the delighted spirit glow,
Till joy denies itself again,
And, too intense, is turned to pain.
For, by permission and command
Of thine own Prince Ferdinand,
Poor Ariel sends this silent token
Of more than ever can be spoken;
Your guardian spirit Ariel, who
From life to life must still pursue
Your happiness, for thus alone
Can Ariel ever find his own.
From Prospero's enchanted cell,
As the mighty verses tell,
To the throne of Naples he
Lit you o'er the trackless sea,
Flitting on, your prow before,
Like a living meteor.

When you die, the silent Moon
In her interlunar swoon
Is not sadder in her cell
Than deserted Ariel.
When you live again on earth,—
Like an unseen star of birth,
Ariel guides you o'er the sea
Of life from your nativity.

* T

Many changes have been run
Since Ferdinand and you begun
Your course of love, and Ariel still
Has tracked your steps and served your will.
Now, in humbler happier lot,
This is all remembered not;
And now, alas! the poor Sprite is
Imprisoned for some fault of his
In a body like a grave:
From you he only dares to crave,
For his service and his sorrow,
A smile to-day, a song to-morrow.

The artist who this idol wrought,
To echo all harmonious thought,
Felled a tree while on the steep
The woods were in their winter sleep,
Rocked in that repose divine
On the wind-swept Appennine,
And dreaming, some of Autumn past,
And some of Spring approaching fast,
And some of April buds and showers,
And some of songs in July bowers,
And all of love. And so this tree—
Oh that such our death may be!—
Died in sleep, and felt no pain,
To live in happier form again:
From which, beneath heaven's fairest star,
The artist wrought this loved Guitar,
And taught it justly to reply,
To all who question skilfully,
In language gentle as thine own;
Whispering in enamoured tone
Sweet oracles of woods and dells,

ARIEL TO MIRANDA.

And summer winds in sylvan cells.
For it had learnt all harmonies
Of the plains and of the skies,
Of the forests and the mountains,
And the many-voicèd fountains;
The clearest echoes of the hills,
The softest notes of falling rills,
The melodies of birds and bees,
The murmuring of summer seas,
And pattering rain, and breathing dew,
And airs of evening; and it knew
That seldom-heard mysterious sound
Which, driven on its diurnal round
As it floats through boundless day,
Our world enkindles on its way.
All this it knows; but will not tell
To those who cannot question well
The Spirit that inhabits it.
It talks according to the wit
Of its companions; and no more
Is heard than has been felt before
By those who tempt it to betray
These secrets of an elder day.
But, sweetly as its answers will
Flatter hands of perfect skill,
It keeps its highest holiest tone
For our belovèd Jane alone.

Printed by WALTER SCOTT, *Felling, Newcastle-on-Tyne.*

PR 5403 S5

Shelley, Percy Bysshe
  Lyrics and minor poems

PLEASE DO NOT REMOVE
CARDS OR SLIPS FROM THIS POCKET

UNIVERSITY OF TORONTO LIBRARY

www.ingramcontent.com/pod-product-compliance
Lightning Source LLC
Chambersburg PA
CBHW031327230426
43670CB00006B/259